Falkland Sound

Brad Birch

methuen | drama

LONDON • NEW YORK • OXFORD • NEW DELHI • SYDNEY

METHUEN DRAMA
Bloomsbury Publishing Plc
50 Bedford Square, London, WC1B 3DP, UK
1385 Broadway, New York, NY 10018, USA
29 Earlsfort Terrace, Dublin 2, Ireland

BLOOMSBURY, METHUEN DRAMA and the Methuen
Drama logo are trademarks of Bloomsbury Publishing Plc

First published in Great Britain 2023

A catalogue record for this book is available from the British Library.

A catalog record for this book is available from the Library of Cogress.

ISBN: PB: 978-1-3504-2701-3
ePDF: 978-1-3504-2703-7
eBook: 978-1-3504-2702-0

Series: Modern Plays

Typeset by Mark Heslington Ltd, Scarborough, North Yorkshire
Printed and bound in Great Britain

To find out more about our authors and books visit
www.bloomsbury.com and sign up for our newsletters.

ABOUT THE ROYAL SHAKESPEARE COMPANY

The Shakespeare Memorial Theatre was founded by Charles Flower, a local brewer, and opened in Stratford-upon-Avon in 1879. Since then, the plays of Shakespeare have been performed here, alongside the work of his contemporaries and of current contemporary playwrights. In 1960, the Royal Shakespeare Company as we now know it was formed by Peter Hall and Fordham Flower. The founding principles were threefold: the Company would embrace the freedom and power of Shakespeare's work, train and develop young actors and directors and, crucially, experiment in new ways of making theatre. The RSC quickly became known for exhilarating performances of Shakespeare alongside new masterpieces such as *The Homecoming* and *Old Times* by Harold Pinter. It was a combination that thrilled audiences, and this close and exacting relationship between writers from different eras has become the fuel that powers the creativity of the RSC.

In 1974, The Other Place opened in a tin hut on Waterside under the visionary leadership and artistic directorship of Buzz Goodbody. Determined to explore Shakespeare's plays in intimate proximity to her audience and to make small-scale, radical new work, Buzz revitalised the Company's interrogation of the relationship between the contemporary and classical repertoire. This was followed by the founding of the Swan Theatre in 1986 – a space dedicated to Shakespeare's contemporaries, as well as later plays from the Restoration period, alongside living writers.

In nearly 60 years of producing new plays, we have collaborated with some of the most exciting writers of their generation. These have included: Edward Albee, Howard Barker, Alice Birch, Richard Bean, Edward Bond, Howard Brenton, Marina Carr, Lolita Chakrabarti, Caryl Churchill, Martin Crimp, Can Dündar, David Edgar, Helen Edmundson, James Fenton, Georgia Fitch, Robin French, Juliet Gilkes Romero, Fraser Grace, David Greig, Tanika Gupta, Matt Hartley, Ella Hickson, Kirsty Housley, Dennis Kelly, Hannah Khalil, Anders Lustgarten, Tarell Alvin McCraney, Martin McDonagh, Tom Morton-Smith, Rona Munro, Richard Nelson, Anthony Neilson, Harold Pinter, Phil Porter, Mike Poulton, Mark Ravenhill, Somalia Seaton, Adriano Shaplin, Tom Stoppard, debbie tucker green, Frances Ya-Chu Cowhig, Timberlake Wertenbaker, Peter Whelan and Roy Williams.

The RSC is committed to illuminating the relevance of Shakespeare's plays and the works of his contemporaries for the next generation of audiences and believes that our continued investment in new plays and living writers is a central part of that mission.

The work of the RSC is supported by the Culture Recovery Fund.

New Work at the RSC is generously supported by The Drue and H.J. Heinz II Charitable Trust.

The RSC Acting Companies are generously supported by The Gatsby Charitable Foundation.

Supported using public funding by
**ARTS COUNCIL
ENGLAND**

NEW WORK AT THE RSC

We are a contemporary theatre company built on classical rigour. Through an extensive programme of research and development, we resource writers, directors and actors to explore and develop new ideas for our stages, and as part of this we commission playwrights to engage with the muscularity and ambition of the classics and to set Shakespeare's world in the context of our own.

We invite writers to spend time with us in our rehearsal rooms, with our actors and creative teams. Alongside developing new plays for all our stages, we invite playwrights to contribute dramaturgically to both our productions of Shakespeare and his contemporaries, as well as our work for, and with, young people. We believe that engaging with living writers and contemporary theatre-makers helps to establish a creative culture within the Company which both inspires new work and creates an ever more urgent sense of enquiry into the classics.

Shakespeare was a great innovator and breaker of rules, as well as a bold commentator on the times in which he lived. It is his spirit which informs new work at the RSC.

Support us and make a difference; for more information visit
www.rsc.org.uk/support

This production of *Falkland Sound* was first performed by the Royal Shakespeare Company in the Swan Theatre, Stratford-upon-Avon, on 5 August 2023. The cast was as follows:

EDUARDO ARCELUS	**GABRIEL**
ALVARO FLORES	**SEBASTIAN/ONE**
SANDY FOSTER	**ROSIE/CLARE**
ANYEBE GODWIN	**JACOB/YOUTH**
OLIVER HEMBROUGH	**GEOFF/DAD**
JOANNE HOWARTH	**MRS HARGREAVES/THATCHER**
AVITA JAY	**SUE/THREE**
TOM MILLIGAN	**JOHN/TWO**
SARAH MOYLE	**MARY/MUM**
LAUREN PATEL	**SALLY/YOUTH**
SIMON RIVERS	**EDWIN/EDITOR**
JOE USHER	**ROBBIE**

All other parts played and understudied by members of the Company.

CREATIVES

WRITER	**BRAD BIRCH**
DIRECTOR AND MOVEMENT	**AARON PARSONS**
DESIGNER	**ALDO VÁZQUEZ**
LIGHTING DESIGNER	**AMY MAE**
COMPOSER	**JACK DREWRY**
SOUND DESIGNER	**ALEXANDRA FAYE BRAITHWAITE**
DRAMATURG	**RÉJANE COLLARD-WALKER**
VIDEO DESIGNER	**DANIEL DENTON**
MUSIC DIRECTOR	**PHIL JAMES**
VOICE AND DIALECT	**GURKIRAN KAUR**
ASSISTANT DIRECTOR	**MARIANA ARISTIZÁBAL PARDO**
CASTING DIRECTORS	**MATTHEW DEWSBURY CDG MARTIN POILE**
PRODUCTION MANAGER	**SAM PATERSON**
COSTUME SUPERVISOR	**SIAN HARRIS**
COMPANY MANAGER	**LINDA FITZPATRICK**
STAGE MANAGER	**AMANDA HILLHOUSE**
DEPUTY STAGE MANAGER	**JEN DAVEY**
ASSISTANT STAGE MANAGER	**CHERYL FIRTH**
PRODUCER	**BEN TYREMAN**

MUSICIANS

KEYBOARD	**PHIL JAMES**
BANDONEON	**MIREK SALMON**
CELLO	**DARYL GIULIANO**
GUITAR	**NICK LEE**
PERCUSSION	**MATT FIRKINS**

This text may differ slightly from the play as performed.

Falkland Sound

Characters

On the Islands:

Edwin
Jacob
John
Mary
Sally

Gabriel
Geoff
Mrs Hargreaves
Rosie
Sebastian
Sue

In the UK:

One
Two
Three
Thatcher

Clare
Editor

Dad
Mum
Robbie
Youth

Acknowledgements

Every conversation I had with Falkland Islanders was invaluable, and I'm grateful to everyone who spent even a moment's time with me. But in particular I would like to thank Matthew Ware, John Smith, Richard Fogerty, Wendy Reynolds, Paula Fowmes, Tony Smith and Teresa Smith for helping me with my research. John Smith's diary of the conflict – *74 Days: An Islander's Diary of the Falklands Occupation* – was hugely informative, as was Neville and Valerie Bennett's *A Falklands Family at War* and Richard Stevens' *Before, During and After the Falklands War*. If our story of the Falklands intrigues you, then I would very much encourage you to read their books.

Thank you also to John Price, whose story began this one. And to Zoe Walshe, our son Woody and my mum Kath for their support and for putting up with my Falklands obsession for the past six years.

I would also like to thank Declan Feenan, Luke Barnes and Kenny Emson for the notes and encouragement. Thank you to Jessica Steward, my brilliant agent. And thank you to Giles Smart, who I began this with. And thank you to Dom O'Hanlon and everyone at Methuen Drama for this book and for the last ten years of publishing my work. Thank you to our brilliant director Aaron Parsons, the creative team, the technical team, stage management, the actors, in the company and in the workshops. And thank you to the RSC, especially Erica Whyman, Pippa Hill and Réjane Collard-Walker, for asking me to think big, for asking me to be brave and for meeting me every step of the way.

[W]e did not expect any one to envy; and, therefore, supposed that we should be permitted to reside in Falkland's island, the undisputed lords of tempest-beaten barrenness.

Samuel Johnson, *Thoughts on the Late Transactions Respecting Falkland's Islands*

Alone, alone, all, all alone,
Alone on a wide wide sea!

Samuel Taylor Coleridge, *The Rime of the Ancient Mariner*

There is no future
In England's dreaming

Sex Pistols, 'God Save the Queen'

Part One

Prologue

The **Company** *enters. They are all wearing clothes that would make sense in a rural British town in 1982.*

They look around, they walk to the limits of the stage. They know an audience is here and they appreciate that an audience is here.

Unassigned lines can be said by anybody in the **Company**. *These are lines that come from the town.*

For tonight we would like you to imagine that this is a town.

And to consider all the things that make up the town.

The people, the buildings, the landscape. But also the feeling of the town. The town's sense of itself.

On the main road is the Town Hall. Near the Town Hall is the Post Office and the Dockyard. And on the other side of the street is the Police Station and the Church.

In this direction is the Hospital and the Football Pitch, and in that direction is the School, and the Globe Store.

Look now as the people of the town start to wake up. Here's Geoff, off to pick up the newspaper.

Geoff   Good morning.

And here's Mrs Hargreaves feeding her chickens before she's even put the kettle on for herself.

Mrs Hargreaves   Good morning, dear.

And here's Rosie! Hello, Rosie. What are you doing out so early?

Rosie   Just getting some teabags. Not that it's any of your / business

Everything is as it should be in the town, everything is in its right place. It all just makes sense.

This town has been this way for a long time. And it's proud of that fact.

Stay a while in this town and you'll realise that community spreads not just through the streets and houses, but back deep through its history as well. As though past generations are as familiar to you as your neighbours, living right next door.

Memories here are stories that belong to everyone.

And even though this town is on an island eight thousand miles away in the middle of the South Atlantic.

Even though this town is the exact distance away from the South Pole as London is from the North Pole.

This town has always thought of itself like any other town in our country. Why? Because it shares an idea with every other town in our country.

This is a story about the power of that idea.

And how, for seventy-four days in 1982, that idea was tested.

This is a history play, but please don't worry, there will still be plenty of swearing.

Listen. The town is up. School has started. And maybe now is a good time for us to begin.

It is March 1982. It's bright but it's cold. Autumn is here. And this is Part One.

One

John   I'm new to the Islands, really. I mean, I'm coming up to my second anniversary but by Falkland standards I've only just arrived. I'm originally from Wiltshire, and grew up believing I was certain to follow my dad into a stale and humdrum career in the civil service. I saw how it aged him, turning as beige and as plain as the wallpaper in his office. One day after leaving college, I spotted an advert by the government to help solve the perennial shortage of teachers on the Islands. It felt like my one chance to escape the inevitable. To be frank, what appealed most was the offer of a fully paid mid-tour leave to travel South America.

Edwin *and* **Mary** *appear.*

Edwin (*reading from the advert*)   The ideal candidate would be a practical, self-sufficient type, who's not shy of adversity or close co-habitation. This is a once in a lifetime opportunity for somebody with good health, a sound mind and a strong appetite for adventure.

Mary   No convicts, no alcoholics and no Jesuits.

Edwin   That wasn't actually in the advert.

Mary   It was implied.

John   I flew in to this tiny airstrip outside the only town, Port Stanley. Stanley is a beautiful huddle of wooden buildings with corrugated iron roofs, painted in the most vivid primary colours. My first teaching post was out on a farm at the other end of the Island, so I was picked up and driven out into camp. Camp is what they call the rest of the Islands. It comes from the Spanish word *campo*, for countryside. Though I'd warn any newcomer to keep their interest towards the Spanish influence on the Island to themselves.

Edwin   The day he arrived the weather was blowing an absolute hooley.

Mary   I looked out the window and I said well I hope he's not big on first impressions.

John *and* **Edwin** *travel.*

John   My driver was the farm manager, Edwin.

Edwin   Wet like the sea had forgotten which side of the coast was hers.

John   Nonetheless he drove the jeep over the terrain at a blistering speed. They don't really have roads in the normal sense, either.

Mary   Imagine a carpet made out of porridge.

Edwin   And that's on a bloody good day. And this wasn't a good day.

John   Despite the treacherous conditions, Edwin seemed compelled to volunteer a rather comprehensive history of farming in the Falklands.

Edwin   And so the first cattle were introduced by the French in 1763. By 1820, there was up to 100,000 cows roaming around East Falkland. During the 1840s, of course, the British government introduced all sorts of incentives to encourage sheep farming, and so my family . . .

John   I drifted in and out. His merciless commitment to detail met with the hard conditions of the drive played havoc with my constitution.

Edwin   . . . to refrigerate the imported semen.

John   Excuse me?

Edwin   Artificial insemination. Not every farm has the equipment to refrigerate bull semen. And it's a rather devilish liquid, see, that wants nothing more than to warm up to spoiling temperatures.

John   I'm sorry, Edwin. I'd really love to hear more, but could we wait until we get there?

Edwin   High winds is something you'll have to get used to, schoolie.

Mary   So strong trees don't bother growing and sheep have legs like iron.

John   I looked out across the vast landscape. Miles and miles of sweeping grasslands, rugged hillsides, hard rock coastlines. What had I got myself into?

Edwin   Best we get you a horse.

John   Is what he said next. 'Best we get you a horse', as if that's a sentence you're ever expecting to hear in your life. But see, horses were still just about the easiest way to travel around. And so there I was, staying two weeks at each farm settlement, teaching whatever children lived there, and then travelling on horseback to the next.

Mary   The fact of the matter is, to survive out here you need three strong muscles. Your heart, your brain and your community.

Edwin   There's a reason there were no native people settled on the Islands before the Europeans. It's far too hard an existence.

John   So then why are you here?

Edwin   I don't know. Bloody mindedness, I suppose.

The farm.

Mary   There's a clear order and structure to the farm. There's the farm manager. Then the foreman, the head shepherds, the shepherds, the mechanics. Then there's the cowman gardener.

John   And where are you in this hierarchy, Mary? Mary is the store keeper, in charge of the settlement's supplies.

Mary   Jonathan, the store keeper is something of a lone wolf. Granted complete autonomy lest they be tempted by the sins of corruption and bribery. My store, quaint as it may seem, is its own Little England. And I, as custodian / must be

Jacob *approaches.*

Jacob   Sins of corruption and bribery, my eye. I saw you give Terry Hanson extra hot chocolate powder in exchange for him massaging your feet.

Mary   Blast you, Jacob. That's none of your business!

John   I taught Jacob for a year before he became the farm's junior mechanic.

Jacob   Apart from the resupply ship and the postal plane, the schoolie's the only regular visitor we get. Even the doctor in Stanley holds appointments by radio and medicines are flown out to the farms.

Mary   And if the doctor recommends anything needs doing then it's up to the farm manager or a person of adequate authority do the, uh, (*does a strangely invasive mime/action with her hand*) administering.

Sally *appears.*

Sally   That makes it sound more dramatic than it is. Anything more severe than rubbing ointment on a rash and the doctor comes out and does it themselves.

John   That's Sally, Edwin's daughter, one of my students and the brightest mind on the Islands.

Sally   Morning, John.

John   Sally's on the verge of outgrowing the farm. I don't know if anyone else can see it, but she could reach for the moon.

Sally   I'm travelling to England next month to visit my pen pal for Easter. I'm making a list of everything that people want me to bring back.

Jacob   I just asked her to not forget about us.

Sally   I'm not going to forget about you, you big wally.

Jacob   And anyway, you'll be back in time for egging season, right? Egging season is the bloody tops. I take the kids from the farm because it's a day out, you know?

John   It's one of the things my family back home don't get. Penguin eggs. They're delicious.

Edwin   People fall into two categories. They either like penguin eggs or they've never had one.

Mary   Your ordinary chicken, fancy as it is, stops laying in winter. And anyway, penguin whites are a dream to bake with.

Edwin   An albatross is a fine egg for hard-working farmers. Good source of protein and I've never met a man who needed two.

Jacob   The thing about egging is you have to creep up nice and quiet, keeping the bird calm and a bucket fast between yourself and their beaks.

Edwin   It's not unlike a hen in how it lays.

Jacob   A hen the bloody size of Big Bird. Problem with an albatross is it gets bigger the closer you get to it.

Edwin   That's called perspective, Jacob. It's not a phenomenon exclusive to the albatross.

Jacob   I tell you what is a phenomenon exclusive to your albatross and that's this bastard who once bit a bucket in half just to get at my nuts.

Mary   Sounds like a lot of work for little reward.

Jacob *approaches* **Edwin**.

Jacob   People reckon you might have some news for us today, boss.

Edwin   They're waiting for me to call the end of shearing season, as that's when my farm holds its two-nighter. The annual shindig. I like to drag it out, though. Keep them on their toes. (*To* **Jacob**.) Nothing springs to mind, Jacob, no.

John   Entertainment is very frugal most of the year so parties like two-nighters are long looked forward to. Each of the larger farms holds their own, drawing in people from all over the Islands.

Mary   A prime fixture in the calendar where everybody makes an effort.

Jacob   For singing and drinking and dancing and drinking with foolish abandon.

John   You said drinking twice.

Jacob   Because there's so much of it!

Edwin   Only reason it ain't a three-nighter is because the human body wouldn't be able to handle it.

John   Is that true?

Edwin   Would you like to try it?

Jacob   You've got your sports meetings, dog trials, peat-cutting contests, shearing contests and your horseback games.

Edwin   Whist drives. Grand-slam bridge tournos. After-hours poker in the cookhouse.

Sally   Dad loses a lot of money.

Edwin   An absolute fortune.

Jacob   And on the second day we do these treasure hunts for the kids. Except we're all in Land Rovers and we're bombing about the place, almost crashing right off the face of the island. It's a laugh I tell you.

During the moving about, **Jacob** *and* **Sally** *end up close to each other.*

Jacob   So people think your dad's about to announce this year's two-nighter. I hope it's before you go.

Sally   It's not the end of the world if I miss one two-nighter, Jacob.

Jacob   It actually would be the end of the world, Sally. Everyone's saying this year's is gonna be the wildest one yet.

Sally   Every year everyone says it's going to be the wildest one yet and every year they're exactly the same.

Jacob   Well it won't be the same without you. Anyway, I should be getting back to work.

Sally   Am I gonna get a kiss, Jacob Price?

Jacob   I guess you are.

Just before **Jacob** *plants a kiss on* **Sally**'s *cheek,* **Sally** *suddenly notices* **Edwin** *approach.*

Sally   Morning, Dad.

Sally *and* **Jacob** *swiftly part.*

Jacob   Have a good day then, Sally.

He quickly shuffles off.

Edwin   Schoolie. You couldn't help me with the peat, could you?

He walks on and **John** *follows.*

John   Because of the lack of wood, every house on the Islands uses peat to burn for heating and hot water. I sometimes help Edwin with his. He's starting to struggle with his hands, though he won't admit it.

Mary   Peat takes an age to dry out, so you have to cut what you need in advance. You're having to thinking forwards, see? So then in the winter you're able to rely on all that work you've done in the past.

Edwin   My Sally's seeing a lot of that Jacob.

John   Ah, is she? I wouldn't know.

Edwin   Don't play daft. Anyway, I think it might do her good.

John   She needs more than a boyfriend to keep her here, Edwin. (*To audience.*) I haven't found a way to tell him, but I encouraged Sally to look at some colleges while she's in England. Unsurprisingly, she was way ahead of me, having already written to a few.

Edwin   Ah, bloody shears are stiff.

John   Why don't you let me get on with this? I've got a free morning and you've plenty to do.

Edwin   Thanks, schoolie.

Mary *approaches.*

Mary   Edwin, you've got to put Jacob out of his misery about this two-nighter.

Edwin   So he's been on at you too? Does that lad do any bloody work?

Mary   It's been a good year. Everyone's worked hard.

Edwin   Oh blast it. Alright, alright. (*To* **All**.) Quick word, gather round. It's almost end of the season, so . . .

Jacob   Does that mean . . .?

Edwin   Yep, a two-nighter. Call it first weekend of next month. Get the word out. Now I don't want to see a single sheep with a tuft on its arse, do you hear me?

The farm excitedly prepares for a two-nighter.

John   The Falklands way of life is unlike anything I'd ever experienced in England. The constant work means nobody gets the chance to worry about the little things. Islanders know their function and their value in the community, and that gives them purpose. Belonging, I think, is what I'm talking about. Islanders just seem to know that they belong.

A raucous, fast tempo barn dance.

Two

The town.

Gabriel   I wake at five.

Mrs Hargreaves   I tend to lie in till about five thirty.

Sue   The alarm goes off at six.

Rosie   At seven sharp I make scrambled duck eggs on toast, black coffee for me and Geoff and milk for the kids. It's a great start to the day.

Geoff   I reckon when people think of the Falklands, they must think of the mountain ranges and the vast stretches of barren land. But I've lived in Stanley my entire life and it's just like any other thronging metropolis of 800 people. Some mornings the roads get so busy you have to use your indicators.

Mrs Hargreaves   I go and say good morning to the chickens. It's all very open here but you have to watch for the bigger birds.

Gabriel   I go for a run along the Ross Road. It's common to see seals and sea lions and even orcas and dolphins playing in the Bay.

Sue   I've got to get the kids, a boy and a girl, ready for school. It's a lovely little community here in Stanley. We used to live in camp, though with my two getting older it began to feel a bit *Little House on the Prairie*. That might suit some but not mine with their behavioural idiosyncrasies, shall we say?

Gabriel   There are many shipwrecks just off the coast. I pass the *Jhelum* wreck as the sun pours out from the horizon. I'm still amazed by how stunning the light is here.

Rosie   The boys have started walking themselves to school. I don't worry too much because it's all very safe here.

Geoff   First thing I do when I get into the workshop is check the jobs list. I could be doing anything really. Repairing this, fixing that. They call me the odd jobs man because I'm odd and I do jobs.

Sue   Michael, my husband / doesn't

Geoff   I'm not really odd, by the way. I just said that for the joke.

Sue   Michael, my husband, doesn't get up till well after the rest of us. He hates mornings, especially cold ones like we're having now. Things are a bit hard for him at the moment but bloody hell it makes living with him hard too. Plus I've got to get ready for work. Plus I sort the kids. It's not like . . . Michael! It's not like I'm his frigging alarm clock. Michael!

Mrs Hargreaves   I open my door and gosh, I can feel winter's on its way. I feel it first in my knees.

Rosie   I'm on nights at the hospital at the moment, so I've a little time to myself. I go for a wander and see Mrs Hargreaves. I say hello and make a little note to check in on her later.

Geoff   People keep an eye out for each other here.

Sue   You're never in want of help if you need it.

Rosie   It's not like if something breaks you can just order a new part.

Gabriel   You don't know when you might need a favour.

Mrs Hargreaves   Oh it's a very close community. Everyone's in each other's business. That's why people here live to a good age. Gossip, done right, is a form of exercise.

Sue   Good morning, I say to Mrs Hargreaves, as I bundle the kids out the door.

Mrs Hargreaves   Do you see Susan there? Well, her husband has recently been laid off work thanks to some mystery illness, and meanwhile she's been having an affair with one of his best friends! Now doesn't that get the heart racing! Hello, Susan. (*To audience.*) The key to my life is routine. Every morning I make it down to the Globe Store. The Cletheroe Brothers used to run it. Joe and Les.

Geoff   Both had been sailors in their day. Like a lot of old folk round here, in fact. You'll even find parts of old shipwrecks down in the foundations of the store.

They bring the Globe Store to life.

Rosie We can take nothing for granted here. So on a trip around the Globe, every bottle, jar and box is savoured. A little reassurance that we're doing alright.

Geoff Every label a work of art. Each description a piece of poetry. I could spend hours staring at the preserves and flavourings and tinned meats and pickled whatever-it-is-they've-pickled.

Sue Imported cakes and biscuits.

Rosie Medicines, iodine, rubbing alcohol, dental floss and toothpaste.

Geoff Listerine mouthwash, Atkinsons soap, ear drops, hair dyes.

Mrs Hargreaves Antiseptic dusting powder for your feet.

Rosie Vermouth, Vermouth Rossi, Calder's Milk Stout.

Mrs Hargreaves Ports, clarets, Sauternes.

Sue Crème de Menthe, coffee-flavoured advocaat.

Geoff And for the courageous there's also the barrel-brewed rum that they bottle in store. Goodness knows what witchcraft is involved in the manifesting of it, but even the sniff of a recently popped cork is enough to render me absolutely stewed.

Rosie Doesn't stop him buying a bottle a week.

Geoff I water it down, obviously. It'd burn right through me and the floor if I didn't.

Mrs Hargreaves Upstairs you have your hardware.

Geoff Tools, horse saddles, oil lamps, harnesses.

Sue Compasses, sewing machines, timber, copper boilers.

Rosie It's always a mess up there, but if you asked for something they know exactly where it's kept.

Mrs Hargreaves   Every tack, nail and button itemised and inventoried with care, and an appreciation that the little things are essential to everyday life.

Sue   A lot of your memories as a kid would be around the Globe. So even as an adult you find yourself walking in with a tinge of excitement.

Rosie   My dad always bought me chocolate-coated Brazil nuts.

Sue   My favourite were these sweets called Empire Mixture, these small flour-coated jellies. Now that takes me back.

Rosie   The Cletheroes have long since retired. But the Globe's still going strong.

A snap back into the present.

Geoff   I spot Mrs H coming. I owe her for some leeks Rosie borrowed for a pie last week. She wants paying in potatoes. But we finished the last of the buggers in the same pie.

Gabriel   The Islands don't have a regular supply of fresh food. So if you want it then you have to grow it yourself.

Geoff   So I dive into my jeep and try and get it going quick. Course the thing runs like an old pig, so I'm turning the key and its snorting and snuffling and before I know it, she's stood right by the bonnet. And all she says is . . .

Mrs Hargreaves   Potatoes.

Sue   Back in the day it was a stubborn hell trying to grow anything yourself what with the sea winds and hard land. But nowadays we use polytunnels and it's quite a fun hobby to see what you can grow.

Mrs Hargreaves   It's more than a hobby, it's a way of life. The Thomson and Morgan seed catalogue is my bible. Along with the actual Bible, of course.

Sue   Mrs Hargreaves, to the wonder of the whole town, can grow the most astonishing tomatoes.

Mrs Hargreaves   The secret is you have to talk to your vegetables. Give them attention and care.

Geoff   She says it's talking but in actual fact it's sheep shit. Covers her garden an inch thick, she does. The stuff is rocket fuel. She has it delivered in the night time because she doesn't want no one knowing she uses it.

Mrs Hargreaves   Potatoes.

Geoff   Alright!

Rosie   Of course you can order things by boat. But you can't always guarantee when it'll get here, so we've learnt to not depend on it.

Sue   We once we had these cherries arrive from England. I'll always remember the kids faces as they tasted them, oh my God. They were a bit soft from the journey, but the kids still loved them. It's the only time I've had a twinge of . . . Are we depriving them out here?

Geoff   Absolutely not. They're learning about self-reliance, determination, pride. They're learning about being Falklanders, in a way.

Rosie   It's hard to not be a bit envious when you get wind of all these newfangled whatnots readily available in England.

Geoff   My cousin's got a Commodore 64.

Rosie   But we're happy here. That doesn't mean it's always easy, but we're content.

Sue   It's no surprise to me, though, to hear the population's falling.

Gabriel   Think it's around 1,800 in total now. At one point it was nearly three thousand.

Geoff   You see a few more people go and you think, well, blast me, the fewer of us there are and the more like sitting ducks we are to the Argentinians. Not that it should be on anybody to stay or nothing.

Gabriel   I get to work. I've been a technician at the Marine
Biology Research Centre for almost a year now. The weather
is biting cold. I can't get used to the seasons here. I'm from
the northern part of Argentina, so this isn't my climate.

Geoff   You get every type of scientist pass through. You get
your boffins and your eggheads and your poindexters and
your geeks.

Rosie   From all over the world people come, yeah. It's an
area of interest because of the unusual habitats and that. It's
nice to meet them. Morning, Gabriel. It keeps us in touch
with the world.

Sue   And it's right as I'm about to drop the kids off to
school when Oliver suddenly chirps up and says, oh, Mum,
by the way, Miss said the trip's cancelled today. So bloody
Nora, that's normal pick-up time and I have to rearrange
my afternoon. Thanks for telling me at the last possible
moment.

Geoff   I said to my wife this morning, I said, do you know
what's happened now? Terry was telling me last night.

Rosie   All the kids in Stanley were due to have a school trip
on board HMS *Endurance*, which is a lovely treat. They do it
every year.

Gabriel   The *Endurance* is the icebreaker that patrols the
Antarctic Ocean.

Sue   But today's been cancelled because it has to go and
sort out the situation in South Georgia.

Rosie   South Georgia is an old whaling port about 900
miles away, it's just an island of seals and rust really. Makes
us look like Manhattan.

Gabriel   It's still important for scientists.

Geoff   And this transport ship belonging to the
Argentinians lands forty-one scrap-metal workers on it. To
dismantle and take away any old scrap they can salvage.

Gabriel   Not that there's anything unusual with that.

Geoff   But that was just a ruse, you know? As soon as they got there they seized the Island and ran up the Argentinian flag.

Rosie   They've graffitied everywhere and trashed the place.

Mrs Hargreaves   It was plainly obvious from the start that they were up to no good.

Geoff   Temerity. That's the word I use for it. Is temerity the right word?

Rosie   People are nervous, they think this is meant to send a message, a warning to us that we're next.

Gabriel   It's undeniable that the mood back home is very hot right now. Things are difficult economically, politically. This can lead to silly, symbolic gestures.

Sue   The argument's always rumbling on.

Rosie   Over the last few years we've been under pressure from the British government to be more friendly with the Argentinians.

Mrs Hargreaves   We're not very keen on that.

Rosie   The fact is the Argentines don't help their case with the way they're going about things.

Geoff   There's definitely been an increase in shenanigans.

Rosie   Like stamping your passport over your photograph so it invalidates the entire sodding thing.

Gabriel   It happens to Argentinians too.

Mrs Hargreaves   Or defacing our mail.

Gabriel   It's for translation. Often the postal service will write the Spanish over the English when processing.

Rosie   Every third or fourth letter will have been opened.

Gabriel   There is a different relationship to privacy.

Rosie   They'd just sellotape the top. As if we wouldn't notice sellotape.

Geoff   The last time we were passing through Argentina, the taxi driver, and this is true now, he said, 'See you soon'. Now what the bloody hell do you think he meant by that?

Sue   The reality is though that we have to find some way of living with them. I mean, if you talk to my kids about Buenos Aires then it's all about the arcades and the cinemas and whatever else. For young people there's naturally a pull to . . . I guess I'm a bit indifferent about it. I went to college in Uruguay so maybe I'm a bit more . . .

Gabriel   When I speak to my family back home, they are always asking me about the English. Like I'm some sort of expert.

Mrs Hargreaves   I've got nothing against them. I'm sure it's very nice if that's what you know.

Gabriel   Then people here ask me the same about Argentina. What are they thinking, what are they doing?

Rosie   No one really knows what's going on.

Gabriel   They try and be diplomatic with me. Like I might be pro-junta. I have to say to them, I left the place for a reason, you know?

Sue   I guess, yeah, this does feel like an escalation.

Geoff   We can get on with most stuff by ourselves. But I do hope Britain have got an eye on this, yeah.

Gabriel   You just have to get on with your day.

Sue   And hope that politics will sort it out.

Three

The UK.

One   Look around you.

Two   Just look around you.

One   Look at your neighbours. Your colleagues.

Two   Your family. Your friends.

One   Look at your doctor. The bank manager.

Two   The postman. The man who cleans your windows.

One   You'll see it in their faces.

Two   Once you notice it you'll see it everywhere.

One   What I'm talking about is shame. Shame in our country. Shame in ourselves.

Three   It wasn't always like this. Our parents could be proud.

Two   They won a war.

One   They should be proud. And we're proud of them. But proud of ourselves?

Two   No jobs, high inflation, a crumbling NHS.

Three   A devalued pound.

One   The sick man of Europe.

Two   A three-day week.

Three   Proud of ourselves? We can't even make a decent car anymore.

One   The Industrial Revolution. That was here in England.

Two   We had an empire.

Three   The world looked to us to show them the way.

One   And now you look at your lot and you look at theirs and you think, hang on. Hang on, we taught you that. We gave you that.

Two   And that's nothing against them but it's embarrassing to feel overtaken.

Three   I remember when England meant jam on toast. Muddy knees. Mum's in the garden. Dad's fixing something in the shed. Seaside holidays. Cricket on the green.

One   Tea shops. Bird baths.

Two   Well-turned-out, law-abiding, church-going.

One   Dogs and cats.

Two   Britishness.

Three   Now look at the books written about our country. They're all called things like 'Panic!'

One   'The End of Britain'.

Two   'Fuck Me, What a Mess'.

One   Our parents won a war.

Two   That country feels so foreign now. So what about us?

Youth   This septic isle.

Youth   Nothing works. Not even the people.

Mum   It gets to the point when I'm just relieved to make it to the end of the week.

Robbie   When I finish school.

Dad   You've just got to cling on to what you've got, look after your own, and wish everyone else well.

Robbie   When I finish school I want to do anything.

Dad   A strike every week it feels like.

Mum   It's not just the strikes.

Robbie   Anything that gets me out of here.

Dad   You just want to be able to put fuel in your car and food on the table.

Mum   I look at Callaghan on the television and he's saying this and that but I can tell. He's got no idea. And that scares me. Actually. If we're being serious for a minute. Heath was bad. Wilson was bad. But Callaghan? Never again will I vote for a politician to solve our problems.

Dad   What this country needs is a –

Editor   A date for the 1979 general election has been announced. Leader of the Opposition, Margaret Thatcher, says she is ready for the fight.

Clare   Margaret Thatcher, the former Secretary of State for Education, is best known for ending the provision of free milk for all children between the ages of –

Youth   Margaret Thatcher – Milk Snatcher.

One   What this country needs is a new direction.

Two   A leader who'll stand up against the status quo.

Three   Who's prepared to administer whatever hard medicine is necessary to cure the disease.

Dad   What this country needs is a . . . I'm good at my job. And I am sick of not having enough of anything. I'm talking about fairness, self-respect.

One   But I mean, a woman?

Two   It's a risk.

Three   Pragmatically, who do you think will beat Labour? Because that's all that matters.

Mum   The thing is, she's a grocer's daughter, isn't she? She's a grocer's daughter so she understands that this country is nothing, nothing without hard work and grit.

Editor   Grantham. They don't make winners in Grantham.

One   They do now.

Clare   Margaret Thatcher has become Great Britain's first female prime minister.

Dad   Yes, I did vote for her but no that doesn't make me a Tory.

Mum   I didn't like the milk thing but, I mean, there's something about her, isn't there? She looks like she has a plan.

Clare   But now she's in, what exactly is this plan?

One   The theory is called monetarism.

Editor   The brains behind the idea is Milton Friedman, the Nobel Prize-winning economics superstar, applauded for his radical approach to public spending.

Two (*as* **Milton Friedman**)   The theory is simple. There's not a lot you can do in an economy. You can either put money in or take money out.

Three   You can put money into the system.

One   That creates jobs.

Two (*as* **Milton Friedman**)   But it also increases inflation. That means the value of your money goes down.

Three   And if the value goes down the more you have to spend on wages.

One   Spend more on wages and your businesses can't keep up.

Three   People lose their jobs again.

Two (*as* **Milton Friedman**)   The only way a government can consistently ensure a balanced economy is to keep inflation low. And that means restricting the amount of money it puts into the system.

Three   Now that does mean people still lose jobs.

One   In the short term. It eventually settles to a natural level.

Robbie   What does that even mean, 'natural level'? You gonna go up to a bloke on the street and say you don't have a job but don't worry, it's the natural level?

Youth   You can't ask a kid to eat natural level for his tea.

Clare   This may all sound very exciting in the *Boys' Own*, warm-aired lecture halls of Chicago. But what about in the real world?

Editor   The prime minster today is expected to make a statement on the current forecast for the worst recession in half a century.

Three   What this country needs is, a, a bit of fucking patience.

Clare   There's no time for patience in a five-year election cycle. She's got until 1984 and then that's it.

One   Monetarism is an intricate –

Clare   Failure.

Editor   What does Milton Friedman say?

Two (*as* **Milton Friedman**)   Unfortunately, actual practice has, uh, not conformed to theory.

Clare   Thatcher ends 1980 with her economic experiment in tatters. She is shadowed by 2.2 million unemployed, bruising fights with unions, Northern Ireland on the brink, embassies under siege, hunger strikes, assassinations, CND marches, industrial collapse and prisoners escaping from Broadmoor. It's four minutes to midnight and Great Britain has the most unpopular prime minister since records began.

Editor   I appreciate the writing style but try to not sound too happy about it, hey? It's good news that sells papers.

Mum   I thought the point was that she was gonna sort everything out. Prices are still going up, people are losing their jobs.

Youth   I've always hated Thatcher. A plague on the house of any idiot that voted for her.

Mum   Well, hang on, love.

Dad   I lose my job in the same week my boy finishes school. You're meant to want to say: 'Welcome to the world, son.' But the truth is, I'm worried for him. I don't know what we're going to do.

Clare   Consider the pain felt by those skilled workers who suddenly find themselves in the dole queue. And next to them the young, the restless, the bored-before-they-were-born. What a band of fellow travellers. It wouldn't take long for resentments to fester. For it to break out into –

Robbie   War.

Clare   Brixton. 1981. Many take to the streets.

Youth   Class war. Race war. Civil war.

Clare   Followed soon after by Toxteth.

Robbie   Moss Side. The streets we kicked about on. The streets we were harassed by police on. The streets we knew, turned upside down.

Editor   We can't get reporters out there quick enough.

Clare   Any city with high unemployment and tension between locals and the police is ripe for –

Robbie   Merseyside.

Youth   Leeds, Manchester, Birmingham.

Youth   London, Leicester, Coventry and Derby

Youth   In each and every site a message was sent.

Robbie   Cars torched, windows smashed, glass and fire and steel and gravel.

Youth   To reclaim our towns. Say no. Reject the Tories. Fuck Thatcher.

Two   We quickly send out Norman Tebbit to defend the government's position. With mixed results, if I'm honest.

Mum   The street lights on our road get smashed out. It makes it feel properly, properly dark.

Dad   I'm all for tearing stuff down, don't get me wrong. But actual violence? No chance.

Clare   This country suddenly feels, could be, is, ungovernable.

Robbie   Maggie! Out!

Youth   Maggie! Out!

Editor   We're briefed that members of the cabinet are preparing for a revolt of their own.

Three   The thing about surviving in this party is you always need to know which way the knives are pointing.

Clare   There are some grave faces around Whitehall.

One   If I may say, this isn't about economics. It's about psychology.

Three   What do I think of when I think of Great Britain? I don't think of interest rates.

Two   What this country needs is a win. It needs a story.

Three   A reminder that this is a country of self-reliance. Determination. Pride.

Mum   Pride, yeah. A bit of pride.

One   Our parents could be proud.

Two   What this country needs is for Mrs Thatcher to remind us that we are those very same people.

Three   It's about remembering –

Dad   An Englishman's home is his castle.

Two   She needs to pick a fight.

One   Pick a fight and win it.

Four

The farm and the town.

Geoff   I'm locking up the garage and this Marine comes up to me.

Edwin   There's a garrison of them up at Moody Brook, thirty of them in all, on regular rotation.

Rosie   They're good with the kids. Part of the community, really.

Geoff   And he says can I lend some trucks to put across the airfield. I say no problem, go ahead. And I think, well, why would you park across the airfield other than to prevent things from landing.

Edwin   Mary reminds me we've got a Marine in one of the cabins. We rent the cabins out, see, and they sometimes use them when they're waiting for their lifts home. Well, anyway we go and look and he's already gone.

Mary   Everything scattered about the cabin like . . . Well, I was about to say like a bomb hit it.

Sue   I'm driving back after doing some land registry work out at a farm. The plan isn't to go straight home. Instead I've planned to meet with Jimmy, see . . . Jimmy's a friend. A good friend. He was there for me when I needed someone and we became close. To be honest I don't really feel comfortable talking about all this. But that's the point, really, of the drink tonight. I'm going to tell him that it's over. I can't keep living with this terrible lie. But then I see this light, and I'm flagged down. It's one of the Marines, he's blocking the road into Stanley. I ask if this is something to do with South Georgia. And he says yes. And he waves me past and orders me to go straight home. So I do. That's all I can do. And I don't get chance to go for that drink with Jimmy.

Edwin   I arrange a meeting at my house and I invite all the senior workers from the farm.

Jacob   I was there too.

Edwin   Jacob was round to see Sally so he was there too.

Mary   It's about seven o'clock and we're all gathered around the table. Then suddenly this almighty roar rips across the sky. Almost shook all the crockery off the Welsh dresser.

Mrs Hargreaves   I hear this incredible noise and everything just starts shaking around me. I think, oh dear, I've muddled up my heart pills again.

Gabriel   I call home to find out if they have any idea what's going on. They ask if it's not just the British worrying themselves. I tell them I'm hearing the planes myself.

Edwin   The Argentinians were never just interested in South Georgia and everyone knew it.

Sue   And I think, God, you know. I hope we're ready for whatever this is.

Mary   Two British MPs visited us once. I said to them, what'll happen if there's an Argentine invasion? What plans have you got to defend us? And they laughed at me, saying . . .

Edwin (*as* **MP**)   Why? Are you an Argentine spy?

Mary   I hope they're laughing now.

John   It gets to quarter past eight and everyone's trying to remain calm. Then Rex Hunt, the governor, comes on the radio with an announcement.

Edwin (*as* **Rex Hunt**)   There is mounting evidence that the Argentine armed forces are preparing to invade the Falkland Islands. I have alerted the Royal Marines and I ask for all active members of the Falkland Island Defence Force to report to the Drill Hall as quickly as possible.

Rosie   And it takes a moment for it to click. Defence Force. That's my Geoff. I look up and he's already left the table and getting into his combat gear.

Geoff   I've been a member seven years. We've done this and that. Basic training. A bit of fitness and stuff. Nothing to prepare you for / an actual –

Sue   Our neighbour Declan, not long retired, is reinstated Superintendent of the Police. We watch him quickly hurry out of his house in his uniform.

Rosie   I've never been so nervous making tea in my life. The terrible reality of it all strikes me like knives. Geoff's going to be fighting alongside Royal Marines. How's he going to aim a gun, he misses the bloody toilet bowl. And then he's gone, out the door, and I could crumble.

The farm.

John   I want to say something helpful. People on the Islands tend to look to England for reassurance. And that need is sometimes asked of me.

Mary   I see Jonathan wants to speak. He often likes to act like a little ambassador from the mainland. Bless him.

John   I'm sure there's a sensible solution to all of this. Neither side will want an escalation. I think the Argentines will turn up and there'll be a meeting at Government House and it'll all be thrashed out.

Edwin No chance. The Marines are going to clean their bloody teeth, don't you worry about that.

John Surely no one's seriously expecting an actual fight over this, are they?

Mary One way or another, that's it with Argentina. No more imports, no more post, no more flights, for that matter.

Sally But I'm going to England next week.

Edwin Not now you're bloody not.

Sally *storms out.*

Mary Why'd you have to say that?

Edwin I've got more to worry about than hurting her feelings, Mary. She needs to wake up and stop daydreaming about England! Jacob, go see to her.

Mary I'll go.

Edwin No. Jacob.

The town.

Rosie I call the hospital and they insist I stay home because they know Geoff is out there and I'm alone with the boys. At bedtime, I explain something unusual is about to happen. But don't worry about your dad, he'll be fine, and just go to sleep like any normal night. And I think, who would with all this going on? And yet, to my surprise, the youngest nods off right away. Sound asleep, he goes. And in a way, in a quiet way, that breaks my heart.

Sue We're trying to keep calm for the kids, but it's hard, you know, keeping up with all their questions. And then we get a call. Michael takes it. It's Jimmy. He says he's just checking in to make sure we're ok. Afterwards Michael says, 'Considerate of Jimmy to call.' And I think that considerate isn't a word Michael would usually use. But what can I say other than yeah? Yeah.

The polytunnels.

Jacob   I go and find Sally in the polytunnels. They're one of her favourite places on the farm because they stay warm no matter the time of year.

Sally   Course this bugger turns up to try and make me feel better, but I don't want to feel better. I want to tear out of the tunnel and rip all the fucking carrots out of the ground around me.

Jacob   But they're turnips and she'd have a job getting them out.

Sally   I don't want to be on this bloody island for another minute.

Jacob   You don't mean that.

Sally   Don't tell me what I mean, Jacob. I'm sick of people telling me what's good for me, what I should be doing, what I should be wanting.

Jacob   England will still be there. You can do your trip once this is over.

Sally   You don't understand. I'm meant to go see a college next week.

Jacob   Oh.

Sally   It's just to look around. But if I wanted to enrol then I don't have long to apply for the next academic year.

Jacob   Enrol?

Sally   I didn't tell you because I hadn't made up my mind.

Jacob   Yes you have.

Sally   Don't be like that. I thought you'd be supportive.

Jacob   Well, I'm very sorry all this is getting in your way!

Sally   Oh, sod off, Jacob.

Jacob *exits.*

Sally   Jacob. Jacob!

The town and the farm.

Rosie   I stay up waiting by the radio for news.

John   Patrick Watts, the DJ, says they're going to keep going all night, broadcasting information as and when they have it.

Geoff   They usually finish at about ten o'clock. They sign off with the anthem.

Mary   But not tonight.

Sue   Instead he says he's going to stay with us, playing his favourite records and taking requests.

*The **Company** sings a choral version of 'Goodbye Stranger' by Supertramp.*

John   Which feels very Falklands in its own way. Mad and brilliantly defiant.

Sue   I look around my living room. It all feels so silly to be sat around. I spot a stain on the carpet I'd never seen before.

Rosie   I think about barricading the doors and windows. How can I defend my boys?

Geoff   We're all stood around in the scout hut. David Morris has brought a cricket bat. What the fuck is he going to do with that?

Mary   I make pots of tea, let them go cold, and then just pour them away.

Gabriel   I pack a bag in case I need to go. But go where? We're trapped on this island.

Rosie   All I can think about is how the uniform trousers pinch Geoff something awful at the crotch.

Geoff   I keep having to quietly readjust my nuts while the Marines gives us our orders.

Sally   My room is stifling. I can't breathe. I fling open my windows and the blast of autumny night air makes me go dizzy.

Edwin   I remember that Jacob's family lives on one of the smaller nearby islands. I say are you sure you don't want to go home, lad?

Jacob   There's nothing out there for the Argentines. I want to stay here and defend the farm.

John   Defend? Jacob, what do you think we can do?

Mary   It's like a dream. A very bad dream full of dread and worry.

Sally   I stand at my open window. I feel like I'm on the edge of reality.

Sue   No one gets a wink of sleep.

John   And then it comes.

The racket of war begins. For the town, it happens close by. For the farm, it's on the radio.

Rosie   Quarter to six and we hear the first explosions.

Sue   Gunfire, crumps of mortar. It's louder than what I'd told the kids to expect.

Rosie   Rex Hunt is on the radio again. He's telling us that Government House is under fire.

Gabriel   A tank rumbles along, it's too heavy for the road. It crushes the tarmac and kerb under its tracks.

Mary   So much for your bloody de-escalating, Jonathan!

Sue   We hide under the table in case bullets start tearing through the house.

Rosie   The boys ask about Geoff. I say your dad's part of the negotiations to make peace.

Mrs Hargreaves   With all this racket I go outside to check on my chickens. I see there's a man stood in my garden. Hello, Geoff, would you like a cup of tea?

Geoff   Get to the ground, there's a bloody invasion going on!

Gabriel   There's a short battle on King Street. I watch it from the window.

John   Patrick Watts is still on the radio. He's putting people live on air, reporting on what they're seeing.

Sue   Houses getting battered by shrapnel.

Rosie   Flooding where a shell hit a water tank.

Geoff   I'm in one of the downstairs offices at Government House. I can't tell which gunfire's which and what direction it's coming from. I don't know whether to hold my place or keep going. I'm not trained for this shit.

Gabriel   Then Rex Hunt comes back on the radio, calling for a ceasefire.

Edwin   Does that mean we've won or they have?

Sue   He orders the men to lay down their weapons.

Rosie   And that he's very sorry this has happened.

Geoff   I hear Spanish voices shouting. A lad grabs me by the arm and throws me into a line next to Dave Morris. He's got blood all over him.

Rosie   And before signing off Rex Hunt swears the British will be back.

Mary   But what does that mean? We're still bloody here!

Sue   I look out my window and see an Argentine flag now flying over Government House.

Rosie   Soon after more helicopters land, and out comes a load of red-hatted Argentines. Some are wearing sunglasses.

Sebastian *enters.*

Sebastian (*speaks a few long, descriptive lines in Spanish, then pauses*)   Your faces. 'Shit, how much of this is going to be in Spanish?' No, I'm kidding, It was a bright, crisp and clear morning. Things had gone fairly well, with minor casualties.

Rosie   I recognise one of the soldiers walking down the road. He used to live here.

Sebastian   I used to work at the LADE, the Argentinian airline that connected the Islands with the rest of South America. It's great to be back. The audacity of the last few hours, I'm very proud. And against the British! Not that I'm anti-British, but it's satisfying to think the world will be waking up to hear that we outsmarted the pirates.

Gabriel   It's common in Argentina to call the English pirates. Referring back to the time of Drake and the privateers, the sense that Britain would just take what they want.

Sebastian   It's been a hard few years for my country. This is a good reminder to our people that we can be strong, we can go forward with the winds of justice behind us as we right historical wrongs. We have a detailed, mapped-out plan of Stanley. Different squads are assigned tasks. My first job is to requisition the radio station. The DJ is still playing. I tell a technician that we have everything recorded on tape.

Gabriel   I suddenly get a thought. I wonder, could these be mercenaries? The whole thing felt so professional and slick.

John   The broadcast continues as the station is taken over. Patrick Watts asks for a gun to be taken from his back.

Gabriel   And then the soldiers all start arguing amongst themselves.

Sebastian   Why have you brought a gun in here? What the hell are you doing?

Gabriel   And I go, ah no, this is definitely Argentina.

Sebastian   I take to the air. I inform the population that they are safe. And that they are now under the jurisdiction of the Republica Argentina. The British military forces, police and volunteers are under arrest.

Rosie   I think, well, thank God Geoff's still here. I'd been imagining he was already on a helicopter to South America by now.

Gabriel   They then play a recording of Galtieri. It's in Spanish and I suddenly feel weird. This is my language, so is this for me?

Mary   We change channels to the World Service, just as the BBC in London are saying it believes the Falklands may have been invaded. May!

Rosie   You can hear them stalling and trying to stretch what little they do know into a full picture.

Edwin   How could Britain let this happen? Imagine if this was London. Imagine if someone just walked up to the Houses of Parliament and did this.

John   But this isn't London. We're in the middle of the South Atlantic. A few islands lost at sea, lost in another time. Or maybe not lost, but in a dream. Oblivious to the world, oblivious to the coming tide. Fast asleep and now bumped, shockingly, awake.

Five

The farm.

Sally   It's been two days since the invasion. It's strange on the farm. Apart from what we're hearing on the radio, nothing has changed.

Mary   I go back to my store and sweep it through. I've swept it on the hour for the past six hours. I'm thinking about everyone in Stanley.

Edwin   There's a lot of valuable stuff on this farm. We've got vehicles, stores of diesel, bikes, horses, rifles, food. Sooner or later the Argentines will come snooping for it.

John   I don't tell anyone but I spend the night quietly packing. It's probably right that I should leave, but I've no idea how to tell them. There's a strange and heavy mood at the farm. People have long worried about Argentina without perhaps believing anything would actually happen. They would almost play with their fear like a cat with a ball of string. But now the ball's unravelled and they don't know what to do with it.

Edwin   I hold a meeting with every adult on the settlement. We have to carry on. The animals still need tending to.

John   I second that. It's good for us to keep some sort of routine.

Mary   Perhaps we could reorganise the work programmes to coincide with the news bulletins.

Jacob   I can't speak Spanish. How are we even going to talk with each other?

Mary   They're not going to make us speak Spanish in our own homes, Jacob.

Edwin   There's going to be a strict rota for who's out on the fields any time. We can't just have people going about willy-nilly. And women should be accompanied by a man whenever they're outdoors.

Sally   That's mad.

Edwin   Thank you, Sally.

Sally   No, I'm serious. Why should women's movement be restricted?

Edwin   For safety.

Sally   It's sexist.

Edwin   We've been invaded, Sally, we don't have time for politics.

John   What if we assigned teams? Then it's less about male, female, and more about being pairs?

Mary   Good idea, Jonathan.

Edwin   Fine. Mary with me. Sally with Jacob. Martha with Cliff . . . (*Notices an awkward glance between* **Sally** *and* **Jacob**.) What? What's the matter?

Jacob   Well, thing is, boss, I'm going to be busy looking after the generators. So maybe Sally should pair with someone else.

Edwin   Fine, Sally goes with Cliff. Martha you're with John. The shepherds . . .

Jacob   Not Cliff.

Edwin   What?

Jacob   I'll be with Sally, it's fine. I'll make it work.

Edwin   No, you're right about the generators.

Jacob   But, boss . . .

Sally   Just leave it, Jacob.

Jacob   But Cliff starts early. Sally's alarm clock doesn't even go off till seven.

Edwin   How do you know what time Sally's alarm goes off?

John   Maybe pairs is too complicated. Maybe we just try and stay near others when we're out.

The town.

Sue   It's been three days and we're still indoors. They keep saying over the radio to stay in your property unless there's an emergency. But it all feels like an emergency.

Gabriel   The soldiers have occupied many of the public buildings. They don't seem to be going into people's houses. Not yet anyway.

Sue   Because of my job I've got files of documents from the Legislative Council. So I start secretly burning them in the Rayburn. Page by page so no one would suspect a thing about our fire.

Rosie   We get a knock on the door and it's Geoff. The soldiers with him search the house and confiscate anything they perceive to be weapons. I don't care. I'm just glad to have him back.

Geoff   The boys jokingly check me over for bullet wounds. I laugh, but really, my hands haven't stopped shaking.

Sue   I start making a tally of everyone who lives alone, who might be isolated. I call them up to make sure they're ok.

Mrs Hargreaves (*on phone*)   Don't worry about me, dear. I'm just dusting and polishing the silver.

Sue (*on phone*)   Well, that's good to hear.

Mrs Hargreaves (*on phone*)   And how are the tiddlywinks?

Sue   That's what she calls my kids. At least I think she means the kids. It doesn't matter, she doesn't give me chance to answer.

Mrs Hargreaves (*on phone*)   Did I tell you about the time my Jack went . . .

Sue   She's told me a hundred times. I don't mind listening though.

Rosie   It's unsustainable keeping us cooped up like this.

Geoff   I wonder about the milkman's cows. They must be busting. Udders like bowling balls.

Mrs Hargreaves   I look out my window and it just looks awful. Tanks and broken bits of road and fences down and bullet holes in cars and walls. They've dug a latrine ditch in the middle of my front garden. There's a boy in there now, waving at me. And I think, well, this is the end of days. Are you here to destroy us? Because that's what you've done. You've destroyed our town.

Sue   There's talk of rationing, whether supply lines will be disrupted. Though we're Falklanders and it doesn't faze many.

Geoff   We've got plenty of food in our freezer. Beef, mutton, trout. Never mind the patch out the back, we've got carrots, turnips, and a round of potatoes still to come this year, save the lot we owe Mrs H. We can last as long as they can, the bloody bastards.

Mrs Hargreaves   My chickens are what's going to see me through. Eggy bread for breakfast. A boiled egg at smoko. Eggs on toast for dinner. Omelette for tea. Egg sandwich for supper. And then all again the next day. And the day after that. I'm not that fussed about egg if I'm honest.

Rosie   We still stick to the radio like glue. The most frustrating thing is having to sit through some crap afternoon play just to wait for the news.

Sue   Worse when it's the football. Ninety minutes of the dross without any news at all.

Geoff   And I'm a Chelsea fan, and blast me one Saturday we're 3–0 down at half time and Rosie won't let me turn it off. Like some kind of perverse torture.

Rosie   I listen to a debate on what Britain is going to do. I actually can't believe they're arguing about it. This isn't politics, this is our lives.

Geoff   People asking, 'Well, do they even speak English there?' I've got a few bloody English words for them. My family's been here four generations. As a favour, mind you. The bloody British government asked them to come.

Rosie   The boys start getting cold. Put another jumper on.

Geoff   We've got one of these, we use gas instead of peat, see, and we're running out. Sod the bloody jumpers, this is ridiculous.

Rosie   Geoff, what are you doing?

Geoff   I'm getting us some fuel.

Rosie   You can't go out.

Geoff   It'll be fine. I made up this peace flag using a tea towel and a broom.

He walks out.

I walk out onto the street, taking my time. And I'm being careful like.

Sue   Out my window I suddenly see Geoff walking down the street with this stick and what looks like a pair of white underpants on the end of it.

Geoff   It was definitely a tea towel. For the record.

Gabriel   Geoff walks past my house, between lines of soldiers. And in his hand he's got a broom with a pair of underpants on the end of it?

Geoff   Tea towel. I almost skid over in my boots. The tanks and whatnot have turned over quite a bit of land and it's muddy, you know?

Sue   I'm looking at the soldiers with their guns and I'm looking at Geoff and I'm thinking, for the first time, I actually get angry, you know? I think, you've got no right to do this to us.

Gabriel   And a soldier shouts out to Geoff in English.

Sebastian   Don't worry. We won't shoot.

Geoff   And he's smiling at me.

Rosie   And he walks up to Geoff.

Geoff   And I grip my broom. And if I have to I'm going to ram this broom right up / his

Sebastian   We asked you to stay indoors.

Geoff   I need to buy some gas for my house. We're getting cold.

Gabriel   He offers Geoff a cigarette.

Sebastian   Do you have a family?

Geoff   Yes. Not that it matters. Does it matter?

Sebastian   I'm sorry for the long wait inside. We had to secure the public buildings. The store, the post office will be open for usual service later today.

Rosie   I can't hear what they're saying but the soldier then smiles and pats Geoff on the back.

Gabriel   And a journalist takes a photograph of the conversation.

Rosie   I call Roz at the hospital to tell her that I'm coming in. I've been worried stiff for the patients.

Sue   Gradually people start leaving their houses. It's the look on people's faces that makes it all feel very real. That yes, this has happened and it's happened to all of us. The kids are impressed with all the vehicles. The soldiers are friendly with them and I don't quite know how to intervene. Then Michael shouts at me from the house. He says the dog's ran out. I think bloody hell, you useless . . . And so I have to start looking for her.

Gabriel   The soldiers are very young and are clearly excited by all this. One says hello to me. His face lights up because of my Spanish. He asks me when I arrived. I say arrived? I live here.

Rosie   I get to the hospital and Roz has got a face like thunder. Soldiers are trampling all over the place. And Argentine doctors are making assessments of the patients. I think, they're not your patients, they're ours. And I'm told there's a British Marine currently undergoing emergency surgery.

Sebastian   I spot Gabriel in the street. A familiar face.

Gabriel   I knew Sebastian from when he worked for the LADE. Now he's wearing a uniform with a lot more badges on it.

Sebastian   I'm a vice-comodoro now.

Gabriel   Do I have to call you sir?

Sebastian   No, I'm still Sebastian. I'm glad to see you, my friend.

Gabriel   I wish I could say the same.

Sebastian   I appreciate it's a shock. (*To audience.*) I remember this about Gabriel. He's what I call an intellectual. He sees the problem in everything. (*To* **Gabriel**.) This will turn out in everyone's interest. Have a little faith.

Gabriel   This is what infuriates me. Everything becomes a question of faith, of pride. (*To* **Sebastian**.) What's going to happen to the Islanders?

Sebastian   They are going to live happy, prosperous lives on our beautiful Island. Listen, I'm staying at the Upland Goose, the hotel. That's where the officers are quartered. Do you want to come over for a drink sometime?

Gabriel   I start to feel uncomfortable with the idea of people seeing how friendly and familiar Sebastian is being with me. I don't want people to think I was a part of this. (*To* **Sebastian**.) Maybe, sure.

Sebastian   You don't sound convinced. You will be! Trust me, my friend.

Gabriel *leaves.*

Geoff   Course I'm not the only one who saw Gabriel talking with the soldier there.

The farm.

John   And then news comes on the radio that Rex Hunt along with his wife and Dick Baker the chief secretary are to be deported.

Edwin   I wonder what that means. Course what's in the news all the time is how fond they are of tossing people out of helicopters.

John   By the sounds of it they've been very courteous so far.

Edwin   Oh, excuse me. Yes they've invaded our country very politely.

The town.

Rosie   We see Rex Hunt and a few others go by our window. They're driven past in the governor's red car.

Geoff   A modified London taxi with the royal insignia on the doors. Very classy if you ask me.

Rosie   Wearing all the regalia that's usually reserved for special occasions.

Sebastian   He's wearing an ostrich-plumed hat, big silver buttons, white gloves and heavy gold chains. And we South Americans are meant to be the dramatic ones.

Gabriel   It's traditional.

Sebastian   I'm not making fun.

Geoff   I've no idea where Rex and them are going. I just hope they're treated fairly.

Rosie   It's all quite scary, actually. Seeing people go. Like we're left on our own.

Mrs Hargreaves   I don't want to leave. I've never been to England in my life.

Rosie   You're not going anywhere.

Sebastian   There is nothing to be afraid of. We are here to give you freedom, to liberate these Islands from imperialism.

Mrs Hargreaves   I just want people to stop defecating in my garden. I don't bother opening my curtains anymore.

The farm.

Sally   A new announcement. Every household has to hand in their CB radios.

John   So that effectively ends any contact between us and Stanley.

The town.

Sue   The flag they put up outside Government House keeps falling down in the wind.

Geoff   I see them struggling with it every morning and I think have that, you bastards. They keep leaving messages for the Public Works Department to fix it, and given I'm last man standing, I ignore them.

Sue   And there's still no provision for the kids. There are only so many activities I can invent around the house. One day Michael comes home from the store. He was meant to pick up some supplies, but instead he brings back a boardgame called Guess Who. I could throttle the useless bugger. Why's it always up to me to do the thinking? Why's all the responsibili . . . Anyway. He's actually been better. He's been good with the kids, and yeah, I wonder whether the invasion has given him something outside of himself to focus on. And in actual fact, we have a real laugh playing this board game for the rest of the afternoon. I know it's silly, but I see us playing this stupid game and think, is this a glimpse of how it could be? And then it's my go and I'm holding this card and he looks me in the eye and he says, 'Have you got a man there, Sue?' I . . . I don't know what to say. But it's just a game.

Sebastian *approaches* **Geoff**.

Sebastian   Excuse me, sir. There is a problem with the heating in the town hall. (*To audience.*) It's humbling to have to ask. This is the nexus of our entire strategy and we can't even get the boiler to work. (*To* **Geoff**.) Do you think . . . Ah. You're the man who needed fuel, yes? Maybe now you could do a favour for me.

Geoff   He stands over me while I do the job, I don't know why, like he's making sure I don't sabotage it or nothing.

Sebastian   Would you be willing to help get together a group of volunteers for a fire service?

Geoff   No one's going to want to volunteer for you, mate.

Sebastian   A fire service is for everyone, no? Fire doesn't care what it burns.

Geoff   Right, that's done. Anything else just leave a note.

Sebastian   Yes, actually the flag outside Government House keeps falling / down

Geoff   See you then.

He leaves.

Rosie   We lost a patient in the hospital today. They were old, and you can't necessarily blame the invasion but it doesn't bloody help. I go for a walk through the cemetery. I sometimes come out here to shake off tough days so I don't carry it back home to the kids. I look at the old gravestones. Some go all the way back to the 1800s. People have been through a lot here. And back then they never had chance to fret. They just got on with it. No, that's not true. I'm sure they did fret. A lot. I guess that's just one of the parts of life that gets lost. All that remains are names, dates and occasionally a cause of death. What about a cause of life? Why doesn't that get written down?

Geoff   We then get some good news. The Rose Hotel's reopening with a licence to sell takeaway drinks, and they can even have the bar open on Sunday.

The Rose Hotel.

Rosie   It's like a wedding party in there on the first Sunday open. People stood arse to back like a sausage sandwich.

Geoff   Everyone's talking ten to the dozen. He's heard this and she's heard that.

Sue   And it just goes to show because everyone's heard something different. And you can't help but think, well, how does that work? Because we're all living next door to each other and we're all getting the same news. I think people just like having something to say.

Rosie   We talk about these new ID cards we have to carry about with us.

Geoff   They let you do your photos yourself. I show everyone I've got a picture of Charlie Chaplin in mine.

Rosie   There's a rumour going round about Gabriel being a spy. Course I don't think it's true, I always got on with him. But how can you know anyone in a situation like this?

Geoff   Let me just say, it's very telling that he's not here.

Gabriel   At this point I didn't realise the Rose was back open. No one had told me.

Rosie   I'm halfway through my second Buck's Fizz and I'm called to help with the delivery of a baby.

Sue   Someone tells me the Argentines have got photos of all Defence Force members. And the addresses of all the people of note marked out on a map.

Geoff   I ask Sue not to tell Rosie.

The farm.

Jacob *works,* **Sally** *approaches.*

Sally   I haven't seen much of you recently, Jacob Price. I'm not used to so much peace and quiet.

Jacob   You're not meant to be out on your own, Sally.

Sally   I'm not on my own, am I?

Jacob *continues to work.*

Sally   I've been making a list of all the things I've been meaning to talk to you about. Like how a chicken got into Dad's shed and laid an egg in one of his boots. Dad only realised after leaning against a hot tractor engine all day and ended up with omelette up his ankle.

Jacob   That didn't happen.

Sally   So you are listening! Come on. Can't be going through all this without my best friend.

Jacob   Suppose we're just getting used to how it'd be with you in England.

Sally   Do you have to be so immature?

Jacob   Yes, actually. Do you have to be so annoying?

Sally   Don't you ever think of the world beyond these Islands? Don't you dream of what's out there?

Jacob   Do you ever think about the moon? Do you ever look up and think about what it must be like to walk on the moon? I'm sure it'd be amazing. And if I went I'm sure I'd spend the rest of my life talking about it like those astronauts do now. But no matter how awesome I'm sure it is, I never sit here and go, cor I really wish I could do that. People get excited about England, but England is a moon to me.

Sally   But England isn't the moon. The moon is lifeless and monotonous and colourless. We're on the fucking moon now, Jacob.

Jacob   No. You're not listening.

Sally   Neither are you.

She walks away and bumps into **John**.

John   Sally.

Sally   I saw you've cleared your stuff out the schoolhouse. Are you going then?

John   Yes, I am. I wanted to tell you first. I'm going to Stanley.

Sally   What? You're not going to England?

John   For a while I thought I should. I thought it would be the decent thing, to get out of everyone's way, to not be poking my nose in someone else's business. But see, Sally, that's what I do. I cover up my cowardice behind an affected English politeness. Really, I've been avoiding things for my entire life. I came here for experience, and to shrink back now, to slip back into the easy humdrum of my parents' life at the first sign of trouble . . . I don't think I'd ever forgive myself. I've an opportunity here to see a moment of history first hand. It might even be the making of me. So I'm going to Stanley. There are more children there so perhaps I'd be more use. The thing is, I'd need someone to cover my lessons on the farm. Could you help me?

Sally   Yeah.

Six

The UK.

Editor   How the bloody hell are we meant to report on the Falklands?

Clare   We're waiting for cables and our print deadline is in hours.

Editor   The locals could be all strung up by now and we're on our arses. Do they even speak English? Is it a colony or a territory? Can we even say the word colony?

Clare   How have we reported on them before?

Editor   We've got bugger all in the archive except travel features.

Clare   Travel?

Editor (*looking through photos*)   Interesting enough to look at, I suppose. Windswept, blustery, a bit Byronic. I prefer a beach in Malaga myself. Have a look. Nothing shouts invasion, does it?

Clare   Why do the Argentinians want it?

Editor   Pride? No idea. I suppose it's closer to them than it is anywhere else. But just because it's close doesn't mean you have a right to it.

Clare   Like us and Northern Ireland.

Editor   Now don't start that.

Clare   We receive some photos of the invasion by wire, presumably taken by Argentine media. There's a bleak matter of factness to them.

Editor   We choose the best for our front page. We pick carefully. The photo needs vehicles, building damage, the detritus of war. Readers need to see it to feel it.

Mum   You don't expect to pick up the paper in the morning and see the word 'Surrender' staring back at you, do you?

Dad   Black and white pictures of soldiers all lined up on the floor, their faces in the gutter. And then the headline. 'The Falklands Taken by Argentina'. I think fucking hell, they've invaded Scotland.

Mum   And I look out my window and I see the pavement like theirs, my little front garden like theirs. And it could be here. It could be right outside here.

Dad   I don't understand how it can just happen like that. One minute you're fine and the next your home isn't your own anymore.

Mum   A very strange feeling comes over me. Like there's a burglar in my house. But I don't know what room he's in.

Dad   And all I can think is Thatcher won't stand for this.

Youth   What's she gonna do? She's probably making a packet out of it. She wants to sell everything else off, why not a few islands in the South Atlantic?

I'm stood in the dole queue and it's all anyone can talk about. Someone jokes, those soldiers coming home will be looking for a job. And I think crap, yeah. I'm gonna make the point in my interviews that I've never lost a war.

Dad   They show a map of the Falklands on the news. Two craggy islands is all it is. They say they're farmers. All very rustic. Shepherds and that.

Mum   Oh I do find the outback lifestyle very romantic.

Dad   Not much to it, but they consider themselves British and that's all that matters.

Clare   Yesterday most British people had no idea of the Falklands. Now they've learnt not only that this timeless and idyllic model of England exists, but it also has a vandal running riot.

Editor   The British public demands that she saves our Islands.

Clare   But what action can she actually take? Diplomacy isn't her forte and it's too late to threaten sanctions. Would she attempt to take the Islands back by force? Thatcher has spent the last three years stripping the military budget to the bone.

One   We can't even call it military anymore. You have to call it defence. Defence isn't a very British word, is it?

Two   There's no longer the appetite for adventures in far-off lands. With half the world celebrating independence days from us, the mood is to decolonise. Soon there'll be Cornwall to Carlisle and nothing else.

Three   We are not the Conservatives of old. Trade is the language. That's how we solve our problems.

Clare   We're still in Belize, though. And Zimbabwe, and Oman and Ulster.

Three   But these are peace-keeping missions, we're not / galivanting

Clare   And how's that going in Ireland?

Editor   Britain had been giving up chunks of its empire, a lot of it much bigger and more useful than the Falklands since the war.

Clare   This government has been sending mixed messages to Argentina. Is it true you've long been in talks with them about a possible settlement?

One   We have been careful to manage the relationship. Argentina is an ally, an anti-communist, free-market, Cold War ally on a continent of very few friends.

Three   The Islanders, who I'm told are very competent farmers, need to . . .

Two   They clearly don't understand the full significance of the situation.

Three   Some sort of compromise, a shared ownership, perhaps, is not the worst outcome.

Two   The fact is, the Islanders themselves want to be British. At a time when not many people in the world do.

One   Who can blame them with those noisy neighbours? The junta is well known to be heavy handed with its own people.

Three   Dissidents disappeared, subversives thrown out of helicopters.

Two   Let's be frank, their government is a historically crazed, hyper-nationalist, economically incompetent, nostalgia-driven boys' club and it's hard to see how any country could function with that kind of . . . I should stop talking, shouldn't I?

Three   Politics aside, if Galtieri ends up slaughtering the Islanders then that's not just the end of Thatcher.

Two   It'll be the end of the party.

The House of Commons.

Editor (*as* **Speaker**)   Order, order.

Clare   The government has permitted for the House of Commons to sit on a Saturday for the first time since the Suez Crisis.

Editor (*as* **Speaker**)   Order! Will the member for Stroud please contain himself!

Clare   As Thatcher left Downing Street to attend, a crowd booed and hissed. This has happened on her watch.

One   MPs line up with furious questions.

Two (*as an* **MP**)   How on earth could the prime minister not know this was going to happen? Are our intelligence services that inept?

One (*as an* **MP**)   Hear, hear!

Three (*as an* **MP**)   For years there have been shameful schemes in the Foreign Office, trying to get rid of these Falkland Islands. The prime minister must demand resignations!

One (*as an* **MP**)   Has Mrs Thatcher even been to the Islands?

Editor (*as* **Speaker**)   Order, please! Order!

Clare   Then comes Labour. An opportunity to deliver a damning indictment of Thatcher.

Editor (*as* **Speaker**)   Mr Michael Foot.

Two (*as* **Foot**)   Thousands of innocent people fighting for their rights in Argentina are in a prison and have been tortured and debased. We cannot forget that fact when our friends and fellow citizens in the Falkland Islands are struggling. We must ensure that the Falklanders' association with this country is sustained.

Three (*as an* **MP**)   Hear, hear!

Clare   The more agitated parts of the opposition are stunned. Foot gives Thatcher a lifeline, playing exactly into the hands of those who believe that the left, yet again, have no answers of their own in times of crisis. Meanwhile, the momentum behind any Tory rebellion is sucked out of the air like candy floss up a hoover.

Editor   Fucks my headline right up. I had 'Foot delivers a kick-in' ready to go.

One   With parliamentary revolt kept at bay, Thatcher now must speak to, and for, the country.

Three   Her tone must be precise, her wording meticulous. An argument for defending the Falklands cannot be a case for empire.

One   This is a cool, modern, Thatcherite reinstation of individual rights.

Two   Yes. An Englishman's home is his /

Three   A new Britain, not engaging with the baggage of the past. But as a sharp, international, rights-driven, free-market land of –

Two   Fairness.

One   Pride.

Editor (*as* **Speaker**)   Mrs Prime Minister!

We see a version of **Margaret Thatcher**.

Thatcher   The people of the Falkland Islands, like the people of the United Kingdom, are an island race. Their way of life is British; their allegiance is to the Crown. They are few in number, but they have the right to live in peace, to choose their own way of life and to determine their own allegiance. It is the wish of the British people and the duty of Her Majesty's Government to do everything that we can to uphold that right.

Editor   The government today has announced that a large Task Force will sail to the occupied Falkland Islands.

Clare   HMS *Invincible* will lead the efforts to push back the Argentinian forces and reclaim the recently invaded Islands.

One   The south coast of England becomes a hive of activity.

Two   Portsmouth, Southampton and Plymouth, arise from your slumber! Your country needs you!

One   Instruments of war, not war, liberation, are amassed from far and wide. Helicopters, armoured vehicles, Argentinian corned beef, ironically enough.

Two   Readying the Task Force has been the most epic, brilliant piece of red-hot spectacle.

Three   Old dockers tell the news that they're proudly working around the clock again. The main roads to the south coast have been clogged like the arteries of a darts player.

One   Requisitioned civilian cruise liners, the *QE2* and the *Canberra* join the fleet.

Two   To make up a total of 127 ships and 28,000 troops.

Editor   We send reporters down to Portsmouth to capture the mood.

Clare   I arrive at the quayside. I was expecting hundreds. But there are thousands of people lined up on the jetties and walls, gathered to wave farewell to the Task Force before it embarks on its 8,000-mile journey to the South Atlantic.

One   Television cameras capture sailors on the decks, waving to their families.

Three   Blowing kisses to sweethearts!

Clare   There will be many out there who will find this offputting. The wrong tone, a vulgar pride in something that just doesn't sit right.

Editor   This day isn't for them.

Youth   No one's asking questions. Why do they need all this weaponry to save a few hundred people? What's the real objective here?

Dad   I'm not ashamed to say, I tear up a bit, yeah. That's my boy in there.

Mum   You see, my parents' generation. They won a war. We have to stand up for ourselves otherwise they'll just come and take what they want.

Youth   Who will?

Mum   The Russians.

Editor   We run a poll. Eighty per cent of the public back the operation.

Mum   Some houses puts up bunting. We've still some left over from Charles and Diana's wedding.

Youth   In the same poll, two out of ten people also want Britain to start bombing Argentina.

Dad   The lads from the dole queue say I won't be buying a single pint for the duration of this war.

Robbie *makes his way forward.*

Robbie   We're all at the railings, waving and laughing. We're like football stars or something, being sent away to win the cup. When I was at school I had to sit there while the quiet ones, the proper boring ones, get told they could do anything with their lives. What a waste, telling Martin Pepperstone he could be anything. Martin Pepperstone was dressing like an accountant since he was twelve years old. I left school and they said I could go to catering college, or do a plastering apprenticeship. I said what, so you think all I'm good for is either smearing stuff on a plate or smearing stuff on a wall? No chance. I said I want to fucking do something with my life. They said, have you got discipline? When I know what it's for, yeah. They said, are you strong? I said I'm strong enough, but I'm no Geoff Capes. Why don't you join the army then, lad? So I did. When someone gives you a uniform and tells you who you are, then it makes you feel like you belong. And here am I, not Martin Pepperstone, on a boat and being waved at by millions of people, already doing the country proud.

Seven

The town.

Sebastian   Preparations are made to swear in General Menendez, the new Governor of Las Malvinas. All citizens are invited to the event.

Geoff   Nice of them to ask.

Sebastian   There will be singing and partying and a very long speech. If I'm honest, I'd be glad to get this bit out of the way. The sooner we can get on with the governing of the Islands, the sooner things can get back to normal for the population.

Rosie   One of the Argentine doctors informs us that we're getting the day off for the swearing in of the new governor. I said, no thanks. Mrs Pitman's kidney stones aren't going to have a day off so I won't either. Mrs Pitman doesn't have kidney stones. She's got a urine infection but I had to tell him something.

John *appears.*

John   I arrive in the town. Some of the streets have different names, Spanish names. New road signs clattered over old ones. I almost lose my bearings, as though I once knew a town that looked this, but not here. I make my way to the schoolhouse, but it's been taken over by soldiers.

Gabriel   I notice John talking with some soldiers. I go over and try to help, to translate.

John   Gabriel explains to them that I'm a teacher and that I'd like to hold classes for the children in the town.

Gabriel   The soldiers like the idea. But he must personally collect each child from their home, and return them after six hours.

John   I tell them the address I'll be staying at. An empty house left by a family travelling the other way.

Gabriel   They say he can take any materials he wants from the schoolhouse.

John   I thank them out of courtesy. And then I thank Gabriel sincerely.

Gabriel   I'm pleased he's here. John and I used to get on when he was posted in Stanley.

John   The house is empty, as expected. Evidence around that they'd packed quickly. A kid's plastic hairbrush left on the floor. I set up the living room as a classroom. It's humble but I know I can make this work. As I move the sofa, I discover a set of three hunting rifles. They mustn't have been found during the confiscation of weapons.

The farm and the town.

Edwin   Because of the lack of contact, we don't know how John got on getting into Stanley.

Mary   He's a smart boy, our Jonathan. A bit naive, but generally smart. He'll be fine.

Sally   I hold my first class with the children. I say we're going to put on a play of the Three Little Pigs. I set up a space to hold auditions, though I make it very clear that I've already cast myself as the wolf.

Jacob   I listen to them through the grate in the cookhouse.

Mary   I go and tidy my store. I find weevils in the flour. I think, you bloody bastards, you're not welcome in my flour. And I laugh.

Edwin   Suddenly there's breaking news on the radio. Everyone! They're sending a Task Force. The British are sending an army!

The town.

Rosie   The news spreads like wildfire.

Gabriel *approaches.*

Gabriel   What's going on?

John   Tonight there's usually a service at the cathedral.

Sebastian   There is some conversation whether it should be permitted. Of course I say it must. Religion is important to all of us. I suggest one should also be held at the Catholic church.

Geoff   I knock on and offer to walk Mrs H down with us. She doesn't even come to the door.

Mrs Hargreaves   No, thank you, love. I'll pray for you from here.

Gabriel   I head to the Catholic church. I'm not religious but sometimes I go because it reminds me of home. But tonight it's full of soldiers. I've never seen it so full. I decide not to bother.

The cathedral.

Rosie   The church is very a special place to me.

Geoff   It's the tallest building in the town.

Rosie   All my ancestors have stood in here at some point of their lives. It gives you a sense of being part of something bigger. It isn't a big congregation tonight, a few people wanted to stay at home. That's up to them, but I'm glad to see so many familiar faces. A united front.

Geoff   We're kind of making eyes at each other, we all know the news. There's a feeling that maybe this sorry palaver will all soon be over. And it'll end up just being one of those things we talk about.

Rosie   I think that's wishful thinking myself.

Geoff   There's no harm in that, is there?

Sue   I look over and see Jimmy and his family are here. He doesn't look back but I know he'd have seen me. Is he angry with me? How dare he be angry with me?

Geoff   There are a few soldiers, watching on.

Rosie   And I think for goodness' sake. Why do you need to be here for this?

John   I join the congregation and stand at the back.

Rosie   This is our community.

Geoff   We were alright here. We were doing fine.

Rosie   This isn't some territory or a bunch of rocks like it's being spoken about. I've got patients in that hospital there, my kids are here.

John   Some people turn and see me. I smile. They all look shattered and stunned. This community has always been proud of the idea that it's self-reliant, resilient and free. The news of the British Task Force may be welcome, but the need to be saved just shows that the idea they had of themselves just isn't true.

Sue   The service begins.

Geoff   We sing and say a few prayers.

Rosie   Just like we always have.

The **Company** *sing a choral version of a prayer.*

Part Two

Prologue

The **Company** *has returned.*

Uh. So when we're ready we'll begin Part Two.

It's another new morning in the town and it's a cold day.

It's winter and it's snowing.

It's perhaps the coldest day of the year so far.

On days like this you'd expect to see Geoff out in the truck clearing the roads for cars.

And you'd expect to see Jimmy and Michael out skimming salt outside their homes.

And then a little later you'd expect children to burst out from their homes all wrapped up warm, keen on building snowmen and sledging down the quiet roads.

Except today they're not. And yesterday they weren't. They won't be tomorrow and in fact they don't know if they ever will again.

Something extraordinary is happening in this town.

It's the end of April 1982 and the town is occupied by the Argentine military.

Everyone is in their own homes.

Looking out at their town, looking out at their town made strange.

You don't expect to see a tank parked outside the church, and yet here it is.

You don't expect to see a garrison of soldiers camping out in front of the post office, and yet here they are.

As though a child's dream of distant wars and adventures has somehow slipped through the barrier of consciousness and made very real on the streets outside.

This is no dream.

And yet it's happening.

This is not meant to happen

And yet it does because it is right now.

And so what of the town? What of the country? And what of the people?

One

The farm.

Jacob   So I had to replace a fan belt on one of the tractors. It's a job that can take anywhere between five minutes and half an hour. So I take the full half hour, you know, because I wasn't born standing on my head, was I? Anyway, as I get on with it I notice this rubber fan belt has got 'made in Mexico' imprinted on the side. And I wonder, does that mean it's Mexican? It's used on a British farm, so isn't it more accurate to say it's British? Now if you'd believe them, the Argentines say this is an Argentine farm these days. So does that mean everything's now become Argentinian? The tractor, the fan belt, the sheep. Are the people? I'm on this thought for the whole job, and once I'm done I go into Mary's store to ask her, because she's got an interesting thing to say about everything, even when she's wrong, do you know what I mean? Anyway, she's in no mood to talk. She's fretting about rationing stock, because our resupply ship hasn't been for a few weeks now, and even though we've got plenty, we don't know how long plenty needs to last. So I take my thoughts about fan belts and I swallow them.

Edwin   The Americans on the farm decide to leave. Just in case their government chooses to back Argentina. Leaves us down a family on the settlement and a worker on the farm. Shame to see them go.

Sally   Dad makes Jacob the chief mechanic for the farm. It's a lot of pressure.

Jacob   I can handle it.

Sally   I'm proud of him. Though he's probably in no mind to hear that from me.

Jacob   I've got Martin with me too.

Mary   Martin's a Welshman. A rum old bugger who could basically do every job on the farm but has the inclination to do none of them.

Jacob   Hilarious he is. One day he comes running into the barn as white as a sheet going, 'It's the Germans! The Germans! They're coming to bomb us!' See he remembered the Second World War, and the sight of Argentinian planes gives him flashbacks.

Edwin   So what did you do?

Jacob   Well, I ran outside to see the fuss. And there it is, this bomber, right, flying low with its bomb doors open like that. Martin's screaming away, 'Get inside, come on'. But I can't move. I'm kind of taken in by it. You know? The size. I think bloody hell. Mouth open like I'm catching flies.

Mary   You could have got yourself killed, Jacob.

Edwin   Ah, there's nothing he could have done. If they wanted to they'd have bombed that barn to splinters.

Mary   Is that meant to make me feel better?

Edwin   It's not long after this Argentinian troops arrive on the farm.

Sally   Everyone's petrified about them taking over our houses. Hiding valuables, wondering where on earth we're going to go. But instead they pitch up in the cow barns.

Edwin   They ask for a run-down of the settlement. I tell them we're a community of forty-one adults and six children set in 100,000 acres with 25,000 sheep. And that we're a free and British people. They don't make a note of that last bit.

Mary   They order me to make an inventory of the store. I halve the number of everything I've got. I say they're welcome to purchase goods but only if we've enough to spare, and at a premium.

Edwin   Next day I'm out cutting peat across the way from the barns. And they're all watching me as I work. I refuse to be intimidated, but my wrist starts to go. And I'm cutting away and the pain is coming up right through my hand up to my shoulder and I say, you bastards, you fucking bastards. And I don't stop until I'm done.

Sally   I hear Dad fumbling at the door.

Edwin   I can't get the key in the lock. My fingers are numb with pain, I can't squeeze hard enough to –

Sally   Dad.

Edwin   Out my way, love. Got stuff to do.

Sally   Look at your hand, swollen as anything.

Edwin   Don't you be worrying about me.

Sally   Come here.

She wraps it in a damp cloth.

The longer you go on pretending nothing's wrong then the worse it's gonna get. What would Mum say? (*Beat.*) You should get someone else to cut the peat.

Edwin   There's too much other stuff to do and the peat can't wait. If we want it dried in time for the harder months then it needs to be cut now.

Sally   So why don't you put the shepherds on split shifts, overlap an hour and put the finishing crew on peat cutting.

That means you'll have four men cutting peat for the whole settlement for two hours a day. We'll have too much if anything.

Edwin   So you've put some thought into it.

Sally   Not really.

Edwin   You know you're welcome to be more involved in the running of things. If you'd want to.

Sally *ignores it.*

Edwin   I said you're welcome to be involved in the / running –

Sally   I was also thinking Mary should move into the farmhouse with us.

Edwin   You're joking.

Sally   I'm not. Daft to have so many of us scattered around in different buildings and it'd be good for the pair of you.

Mary *appears.*

Mary   I'll only agree if he stops thinking every bit of cloth is something to wipe his hands on. The muck he trails about with, the grubby bugger.

Edwin   Well, don't you be thinking you can come into my house and drain my hot water. I see your bloody boiler going day and bloody night.

Mary   Excuse me!

Edwin   In my house we have a strict rota on the bath / and you're not –

They wander off arguing.

Sally   It's been fun with the young'uns. I'm more like an aunty looking after nieces and nephews than I am any kind of teacher, but we fill our days. It's hard to not feel resentful about the fact I'm meant to be in England. But this is their childhood, and they can't be doing with me dwelling on that. So you have to get used to carrying two feelings at once. The perfect wish buried deep, and the acceptable compromise on the surface. When I was their age I used to try and hide books in my pillowcases so I could read in the night. But Mum always knew because they obviously made my pillows heavy. When you hide something inside another thing, it makes them heavier. It's obvious for pillows and books, but the same's true for feelings too.

The town.

Geoff   You feel a pride, a defiant pride, in cracking on. An ability to endure is part of our history. Part of our character. Rosie starts baking bread, which on the one hand keeps her busy. But on the other, she's not very good at it.

Rosie   I check in on Mrs Hargreaves. Through the door she says she wants to be left alone, which is odd for her. She was such a people person.

Geoff   Her curtains are always closed. I don't like that we can't get a look of her, see she's alright for ourselves.

Rosie   I have to tend to her chickens otherwise they'd be long dead. I can't believe she'd mean to neglect them.

Mrs Hargreaves   When I was a little girl people in town had their own cows for milk. Some had a bull too. And they'd just roam around the backs of the houses. You'd ride a cow but you wouldn't ride a bull. I sometimes see their shadows now pass by my window. There's Molly Brae. Hello, Molly. Now then. I haven't thought about Molly Brae in years.

Gabriel   I get a call from my bosses at the university. They're based in the States, so they're way out of it. Good news, they say. We can keep paying your salary for the whole time the Research Station is closed. Just sit tight and wait it out. This is not the blessing they think it is. Without anything to do, without a routine, I'm fraying at the edges. I

see people like Geoff and Rosie and John still so busy and I
envy them. To be alone with your thoughts for so long it's
not healthy. I'm starting to dread calls from home. My
mother has a way of talking, what *we* are going through, how
we are coping. I want to say, 'But it's not we. You are not
here.' But I don't. I just wait for the pauses to go 'yeah' or
'well, let's see' depending on the tone of her voice.

Sue   I still hear the dog barking at night. I take about half
an hour every day to look for her, even though by now it's
surely hopeless.

John   Whenever I listen to the news from Britain, I'm
struck by how attached they are to the idea of this place.
How important it is for it to continue. I wonder, well, what's
it to you really? I remember in my interview for this job, the
woman explaining to me how this place is British. I thought,
well, it's not really, is it? I mean, not technically. I now realise
that Britain isn't just a place, it's an idea. And it's understood
as much through the myths of King Arthur and the stories of
Dickens as it is anything else. And even its realities, like the
Second World War, are quickly turned into stories so that
they belong to everyone. It doesn't matter if Britain can't see
the Falklands. They imagine it. I wonder how much the
people here understand that. This is an imaginary kingdom
waiting for an imaginary saviour. I think on this as I drop
the kids home for the day. (*To* **Sue**.) It doesn't seem to matter
what work I set the children, Olly always seems to only want
to write about the soldiers.

Sue   Can you blame him? We're all trying to make sense of
what's going on.

John   I guess so. I'm just worried he's becoming a bit
fixated. Can we keep an eye on him?

Sue   Later on I talk with Michael about it. We make a plan
to not mention the occupation in daytime hours. Let home
be some kind of sanctuary for the kids. It's good to actually
work together on something and come up with a solution.

Gabriel   The next day a new edict is introduced. Cars are to now drive on the right-hand side of the road.

Geoff   They ask me to repaint the roads. You know, white lines and arrows to help direct people onto staying on the correct side. Now I'm not saying I'm aiming to cause deliberate confusion but I certainly am not doing my job to the best of my abilities.

Sebastian   There is a fundraiser at home. A big telethon to raise money for the Malvinas Argentinas Patriotic Fund. Our generous public are asked to donate things. Clothes, jewellery, anything of value. There are celebrities and even Maradona donates a watch. Our people raise a fortune. We look forward to seeing the results of this, our provisions are running low and we need resupplies. There's only so many times our cook can stew the same sheep head.

The Rose Hotel.

Geoff   One night we're in the pub and Gabriel comes in.

Gabriel   I'm not much of a drinker. But John convinces me that this is a good idea.

John   I grab us a table by the window. I'm not an idiot, I know what people think, but if they just relaxed they'll realise he's still the same guy they knew a few months ago.

Geoff   Now just to be clear, I've never had a problem with him. Never once have I made a thing out of him being Argentinian. But what, are we meant to pretend that this isn't happening?

Rosie   It's nobody's fault but just means none of us feel comfortable talking. In the same way, I mean.

Gabriel   They don't want me here.

John   Just finish your drink.

Geoff   I get it. If I were in his shoes, I wouldn't feel welcome either. Even if I was. Which he is. This isn't our fault.

Gabriel   I do as John asks and then I go.

Sue   I pass Jimmy on the way to the Rose and all I can think is, oh I'm glad Michael didn't bother coming because then we'd have had to stand around and chat. But because it's just us two. We don't even say hello. It's not fair to resent him, but now I do. All Jimmy is to me is a knot of guilt, regret and danger. Danger actually, yeah. And I guess he must feel the same about me. He should do.

John   I look over at Gabriel's empty glass and think, well, Christ, that was a bad idea. Of course now the atmosphere's perked right up. So much for community. So much for togetherness. Cheers!

Others, not knowing the context, 'cheers' back as **John** *downs his drink and leaves.*

Sue   I go up to the bar and ask for a pint. Geoff asks if I've found my dog yet. I say no, and I hear someone say, have you checked round Jimmy's. And people laugh.

Geoff   I laugh along but I don't get the joke.

Sue   And I try and let it go. But I can't. So I leave.

Rosie *follows* **Sue**.

Rosie   Sue, hang on.

Sue   They can't keep their bloody noses out of anything.

Rosie   Listen, Geoff's still got half a bottle of rum from the Globe. He'll be out for hours. Why don't you come round? We haven't had a proper catch-up in ages.

Sue   No. I want to go home.

Rosie   How are things at . . .?

Sue   Fine. Good. Michael's doing much better actually. Make sure you tell that lot, won't you? I'm sure they're desperate to know.

Rosie   We're all here for each other, Sue. Everyone cares, even if sometimes they sound like / they're –

Sue (*interrupts*)   What if I don't want them to care? Can't some parts of my life just be my own? Is that too much to ask?

John   There's a notice put up outside the town hall saying that there will be a public meeting.

The town hall.

Sebastian   So that we can explain the future of our Islands. (*To* **Islanders**.) Soon we shall have colour TVs and Citroen cars available to purchase. As well as more variety of fruits and vegetables. Alongside this there will be some Argentine laws introduced, to make us consistent with the mainland. Such as all people who married after 2 April 1982 would not be permitted to divorce.

Geoff   Bloody hell. Not that I'd want to, anyway.

Sebastian   And all children will be taught in Spanish. Teachers would be brought over from the mainland as they would be more suitable to the task.

John   They then open the floor to us, and it quickly becomes a referendum on the occupation.

Geoff   Mrs Hargreaves's front garden stinks like a bloody zookeeper's boot.

Sebastian   I'll see to it.

Sue   I'm questioned at gunpoint at least once a day. Even when I have the kids with me.

Sebastian   I'm very sorry about that.

Rosie We have strict laws about the importing of livestock here and your Alsatians could be passing on any sorts of diseases.

Sebastian I can assure you that they are very clean.

Rosie It's not about cleanliness, they're a foreign species.

Loud murmuring and disquiet.

Sebastian Listen, everyone. Please. We have to find a solution together. We are trying to make life easier for you.

Rosie That's a lie. This isn't for us.

Sebastian Access to the mainland means fresh food, more trade, support.

Geoff We don't want support.

Sebastian So you'd rather be isolated, all alone on the continent?

Sue We'd rather be British.

Sebastian They have been trying to get rid of you. Look around you. Take the flags away and what of this is British?

Rosie Us. We are. My family goes back here to before Argentina was even made a country. No one was displaced apart from the Spanish who were here the same reason the English were. I'm British, and so is my family.

Sebastian But, madam, what if you're not? So what then?

John But what if you're not? It's a thought I've been wondering myself, but to see it asked to a room full of real people . . . Is it really that straightforward?

Geoff Are you preparing for war?

Sebastian We are determined to defend our Islands.

The meeting bursts into a frenzy.

Geoff Defend! These Islands aren't yours to defend!

Rosie   You're going to turn our home into a war zone.

Sue   What about our children?

John   Soon after, the BBC announce an exclusion zone around the Islands as of 4 o'clock Monday morning.

Rosie   We start having meetings in the hospital to discuss what to do with the patients.

Sebastian   We tell the people that they must be prepared for air raids and blackouts. A curfew is put into place.

Sue   I try and make a game out of blacking out our windows. Olly asks to paint his with shoe polish. I actually let him, because why the hell not?

Rosie   We nail the kids' old favourite blanket to the window frame.

Geoff   It's only when we're halfway through the job does it strike me. Today's meant to be the May Ball. Completely passed me by.

Sue   The May Ball. Used to love the opportunity to get dressed up.

Geoff   Tykes like us wouldn't get invited to the actual thing itself. That was all for Government House types, you know? But Mum would go because of her work, and Dad would let us drink and watch the fireworks.

Sue   It was at a May Ball where Michael first asked me out.

Rosie   Feels a world away now.

John   Put enough pressure on any object and eventually it'll warp out of shape. It's true of the human imagination as it is anything else. What little conversation we do have feels increasingly anxious and paranoid.

Rosie   I start thinking about the people who were sent home. I'm very concerned about it, John. How do we even know they got there?

John   They sent messages over the radio.

Rosie   As if they can't be faked.

John   Rosie, what do you think happened?

Rosie   Think? I don't think anything. I *know* they're assassinating people.

Geoff   They temporarily close the Public Works Department. And I'm bored as old biscuits in the house. I'm not used to sitting around.

Rosie   He's not sitting around. He's fiddling and faffing with everything. Said he heard a hiss on the tape player this morning, now that's in pieces on the kitchen table.

Geoff   The snow on our pathway's looking a bugger, so I decide, sod this, I'm gonna shovel it. I immediately start getting all these looks from the soldiers. But do I stop? Do I bugger! Anyway I keep going and they straddle up to me, close like. And they go, 'We know you were in the Defence Force. And we know you deliberately did a poor job on the roads.' And they look at my Charlie Chaplin ID and they say, 'Do you think you're a funny man?' And I want to say, 'No, just funny looking.' But I don't. I'm actually shitting myself. And they tell me if I keep drawing attention to myself then I'll have to leave Stanley. And I think to myself, hell, I'm going to be put on a helicopter and disappeared into Argentina. So I say I'm not a funny man. And they laugh at me. And I'm angry that they could just intimidate me like that. I don't tell Rosie.

The farm.

Edwin   I'm out putting up barbed wire across the farm. Just to make life that bit harder for the Argentines. Then all of a sudden I drop the mallet on my foot.

Mary   I hear the scream from my store.

Edwin   The pain's so intense I'm not sure whether the whole foot is going to come off with my boot. I brace myself, start undoing the laces, and then I feel this hand grab me.

Mary   I see a soldier stood over Edwin and I think, oh God, he's shot him. But then he calls for me for help and we take him into the kitchen.

Edwin   Mary and the soldier start seeing to my broken foot.

Mary   Suspected break. Maybe a toe.

Edwin   The lad starts talking in this American English. I want to tell him I've had bigger breakfasts than you. No, I've had bigger things for breakfast than . . . No, I've had my breakfast and I . . . Anyway, the pain is making it too hard to think straight but I want him to know I'm not scared of him.

Mary   He can't be older than twenty. The way the uniform hangs off him, he reminds me of Jacob. He tells us the troops were split on whether the British would actually come or not. But now everyone knows and yet he says they're still celebrating at home. And he laughs and he lights a cigarette.

Edwin   And we see his hands are all chapped and bloody.

Mary   Some celebration for us, he says.

Two

The UK. The **Company** *sings a choral version of 'Gold' by Spandau Ballet.*

Three   Just picture it. A destroyer, streaming through the South Atlantic. The Union Jack fluttering, whipping in the wind. And the sky is blue and the sea is blue and pow, you know? Fucking pow.

One   It's a pity we can't broadcast the whole thing.

Two   But in a way we don't even need to broadcast it. It's beamed directly into the imagination of the entire country.

Three   Every single defence cut, and they weren't cuts, by the way, I'm just mirroring your phrasing back to you, were entirely justified. But yes I admit, this is stirring stuff!

One   The commanders of the Task Force are hailed as heroes before a single shot is fired.

Two   Because it is heroic. You have to remember, in terms of sheer numbers, we're the underdogs here.

Editor   Giddy headlines skit across the tabloids. Blast them! Down the junta!

Clare   Before I left, staff in the office had started wearing sailor's hats.

The **Editor** *pops a hat on.*

Editor   The paper expresses itself in a way that connects with the patriotic instincts of our readers. I'm not ashamed of that.

Mum   It's the people I feel for. They're all the way out there and they've no idea how much we're worrying about them. I just want our boys to bring them home safe. Well, I don't mean home. Let them stay there. I hope our boys let them stay there. Safely. And Britishly.

Two   The *Sun* newspaper sponsors a missile. 'Stick it up your junta' written up the side.

Three   To Galtieri's Gauchos with love from the *Sun*.

Dad   I mean it's a joke, isn't it? You've got to be allowed to laugh at a joke. It's British spirit.

One   Privately, Mrs Thatcher is terrified.

Three   But publicly, she's nothing of the sort. She grew up in the shadow of the Second World War. The Britain of her childhood had Churchillian spirit woven into its very metabolism. She has to show the country a strength of character that measures up to the moment.

Thatcher   Do you remember what Queen Victoria once said? 'Failure? The possibilities do not exist.' That is the way we must look at it. And we must go out calmly, quietly to succeed.

Editor   The Task Force reaches the South Atlantic.

Clare   I'm onboard the *Canberra*. With the hard equatorial sun beating down and the promise of war on the horizon, the troops are surprisingly sanguine. Aided perhaps by the fact the flight deck is currently used for sunbathing. I ask a young soldier what the mood is like among his unit.

Robbie   We all read the papers before we left. We know what the country expects. I just hope we're home in time for the World Cup.

Clare   Many of the troops served in Northern Ireland and have been on the wrong side of public opinion. Bloody Sunday was only a decade ago. A lot of these men were boys then. And next to them are boys now. (*To* **Robbie**.) Do the more experienced soldiers have any advice for you?

Robbie   Don't find yourself having to make a decision you haven't planned for. Just do your job and get out.

One   Do your job, exactly.

Three   For the country.

Robbie   For your survival.

Clare   A team of commandos swiftly recapture South Georgia.

One   A clean, precise and technical operation. With only one Argentinian casualty.

Thatcher   Just rejoice at that news.

Three   We start preparing the country for victory. Because really, when you think about it, the Falklands represents –

One   What the Falklands means for our country –

Three   The Falklands are important to us because –

Two   With these foundations, just imagine how incredible our country will be in, say, forty years time.

Three   It'd be easy to say that it's just Argentina. A tinpot junta who've never fought a war. But that would miss the point.

Clare   Soon after, the Argentine Navy closes in.

Three   An urgent request comes in. Two Argentine ships have been detected.

Clare   Just outside the 200-mile exclusion zone.

Two   Believed to be the beginnings of a pincer movement, in a position to launch a raid against Britain's aircraft carriers.

One   One of them, the *Belgrano*, is an old and powerful cruiser.

Clare   Thought, in actual fact, to be turning around. The bad weather jettisoning any planned operation.

Three   The direction of an enemy ship is irrelevant. What counts is their potential, what we believe to be their future intentions.

Youth   The potential.

One   A British submarine has her on target.

Youth   What we believe.

Two   Permission is sought from the prime minister to sink it.

Youth   So many decisions.

Three   Granted. Ready to engage.

Youth   Made on assumption.

One   Confirmed and destroyed.

Clare   323 sailors killed. A third of them conscripts.

One   The British press go haywire.

Editor   Gotcha! Our lads sink cruiser. Stick it up your junta.

Youth   The deaths of young people is nothing to celebrate.

Dad   They'd be cheering if it were the other way round, you mark my words.

Clare   It marks the end of any hope that there may yet be some climbdown, some peaceful resolution.

Three   A nagging fear does creep in. A fear not that we might lose, but that we might win too heavily.

One   We can't manage another Northern Ireland. Britain can't be at the dealing end of a massacre in the 1980s.

Thatcher   Mr Speaker, sir, there was clear aggressive intent on the part of the Argentinian fleet.

Three   There's pressure from the Americans to compromise. This doesn't have to be a pasting.

Thatcher   Had we left it any later it would have been too late, then I might have had to come to the House with the news that some of our ships had been sunk.

Youth   I spot some new graffiti at my bus stop. 'Fuck off Argies'.

Mum   Well I like to keep up to date with this Falklands business, but yes it does get me quite antsy.

Youth   Everyone's glued to the news. Becoming experts on everything. Crime, politics, the financial markets. It's information overload.

Mum   I almost bumped into somebody in the car the other day. I'm sure it was because of the war.

Clare   4 May 1982.

Two   An Argentinian missile hits the British destroyer HMS *Sheffield*.

Three   Twenty soldiers killed. The destroyer fatally damaged.

The **Editor** *takes off his sailor's hat.*

Clare   I wire back a series of interviews. One from a recruit whose brother was on board the *Sheffield*.

Editor   It takes me a few days to read, yeah.

One   The casualty figures aren't immediately released.

Two   So the scale of the disaster is left to the imagination.

Thatcher   Our hearts go out to all those families who have men in these ships. But despite these grievous losses, neither our resolve nor our confidence is weakened. We know the task that faces our fighting men. They are now established on the Falkland Islands, and although they still face formidable problems in difficult terrain with a hostile climate, their morale is high.

Mum   I think she did very well. You want to find a way to pay your respects, but you can't. So.

Dad   Every man and boy who signed up knew what they were going into. So I'm not upset, no. I'm proud. And I know I'm saying that, and I know I'm lucky because the ship my boy's on is never in the news. But I like to think that . . . if he, if something were to happen . . . he would know how proud we are.

Three

The farm.

Jacob   We still listen to the World Service, but it's harder with the soldiers on the farm.

Sally   We hear that talks between Britain and Argentina have broken down again. So we prepare for war.

The town.

Sue   The radio says one thing, the Argentines another. Even with the *Belgrano*. They try and tell us that it just –

Sebastian   Disappeared from radar.

Gabriel   Is that what it will say on their gravestones?

Geoff   In better news, we finally get a decent yield of potatoes. I take some over to Mrs H. The place is looking at tip. I knock on the door but she's still not answering. I want to boot the thing in but I don't want to give her a heart attack. Mrs H!

Mrs Hargreaves   I don't have time today, sorry. My boys are visiting and I've got so much to sort. Jack, Ja-ck! He must still be at work. I hope he's not forgotten to pick up the goose.

Geoff   I can hear her mumbling and pottering about. At least she's up and mobile. I'm about to leave the potatoes on the porch when I notice the chicken coop is empty. Inevitable, I suppose. Sad though too, yeah. I leave the potatoes by the door, knock again, 'Potatoes for you, Mrs H.'

The farm.

Mary   The resupply boat still hasn't arrived. I worry about my little England. When it's bare I realise how twee and sparse it actually is. I'm determined to stay open. I have a responsibility to stay open. But I'm getting tired. There's more air activity in the night times. Bombing exercises, we think it. And I can't sleep a wink.

Jacob   We start trying to find alternatives for fuel. And I only ever have one of the generators going at a time.

Edwin   That means no more baths.

Sally   Yes it does mean baths. Are you not having baths?

Edwin   We take the horses out for shepherding because they don't take fuel like the quadbikes do.

Sally   But it's always a worry whenever anyone goes out because we know they've been laying mines out there.

Edwin   Not lost a sheep yet. Or a shepherd.

Jacob   I find Sally and I give her the chocolate I'd been saving from my ration. I don't like it, see, and I don't want it going to waste. I'm doing it for Mary, really.

Mary   I hear a right load of racket early one morning.

Jacob   The Argentines suddenly start packing up.

Sebastian   The troops are sent westwards, towards where the British have landed.

Mary   The soldier who helped Edwin comes and says goodbye. He seems a little subdued, doesn't meet my eye. I know why he doesn't. Because it's different now. And I look at his gun and I think how dare you. To me he's no longer a chatty young lad but an aggressor, a thug, a vandal. And I know he was kind to Edwin. But that doesn't matter anymore. A gun makes it not matter anymore. And I hope he gets scared. And I hope he gets intimidated. And I hope he gets shot at. I don't mean that. Yes I do. I wish I didn't but I do.

The town.

Gabriel   Some soldiers still haven't got used to the snow. They've been here for weeks, and they're still losing their footing and slipping over. And if they're not then they're sat around, starving and struggling against the cold. These boys are meant to be ready to fight a war now.

John   People start building bomb shelters. There's a rush to buy materials. A near constant stream of people going to and from the Globe Store, carrying sheets of plywood or hardboard, or anything that might do. I'm struck by how quiet and orderly it all is. Gone are the half-hour chats outside the Globe, gone is the nosiness in each other's business.

Geoff   I convert the crawl-space under the house. I re-enforce the load-bearing walls and put a bit of lino down for comfort. There's even enough room for a couple of chairs and if I've time I'll dig a bit further down, then we'd have space to –

Rosie   Geoff, we don't need a bloody en suite down there. It's big enough. Go and help the neighbours.

Geoff   Go and help the neighbours. Go on, go and sort everyone else out, Geoff. Just because I'm a bit handy it doesn't mean I'm responsible for other people. You've got to take responsibility for yourself, you can't always be relying on Geoff. Good old Geoff. Let's all have a laugh at Geoff. Until you need him that is. Well, you're not laughing now. Then again. I wouldn't be able to live with myself if something were to happen. So sodding hell, course I've got to help. And I go through the house and out of nowhere I hear this clucking. What's that?

Rosie   I've been trying to find a moment to tell him.

Geoff   And there's seven chickens in the toilet. I say to Rosie, what are seven chickens doing in the toilet?

Rosie   Do you recognise them?

Geoff   What do you mean recognise them? They're chickens.

Rosie   I picked them up from Mrs H's this morning. They were freezing to death out there.

Geoff   The boys go bonkers.

Rosie   Geoff doesn't.

Geoff   They better not stink the place out.

Rosie   No worse than you do already, love. (*To audience.*) I make a final request for Mrs Hargreaves to be moved to the hospital. But it's rejected. Half because they're needing to keep room for the inevitable influx of soldiers. And half because they think moving her might disorientate her. She's fine in the house, says Roz.

Gabriel   Out on the street a soldier comes up to me, and asks me for food. I say, I beg your pardon? Then I see fear in his eyes, like he's misjudged this and maybe that I'll inform his superior. I tell him to relax and wait for me. I give him bread and cheese.

Rosie   Begging is becoming a problem. Stealing too. It's alarming for everyone. Things are thinning out at the Globe Store. We're on our final packet of biscuits.

Sue   We share our tea with a couple of the soldiers who were parked out front of our house. Daft as it is, I felt sorry for them.

Geoff   Seeing more burials, more crosses being made, you know.

John   There's a soldier dead in the street from exposure. Frozen in place, as if looking back at me, making a quiet mockery of my foolish wish to witness history. It's now too late for me to go home, and too late to not see what I've seen.

Gabriel   I find Sebastian. I say to him that he has to do something about the soldiers begging for food.

Sebastian   It's in hand, my friend.

Gabriel   So they're going to be properly fed?

Sebastian   You leave the strategy to the experts.

Gabriel   This is happening to all of us.

Sebastian   And your patience is appreciated.

Gabriel   My family believe some great victory is at hand. Does it not worry you that they've no idea what's going on?

Sebastian   It's important that people back home have a reason to feel proud. They're paying for this, after all. I don't expect you to understand the nuance of domestic politics. You've been away for a long time.

Gabriel   Can you not see why, Sebastian?

He moves away. **John** *is there.*

Sebastian   A new edict. Any soldier caught begging for food will be shot.

Gabriel *stops walking.*

John   I drop Sue's kids off at their house. We've always known at some point I'm going to have to stop the school. And today I'm telling the parents that this is it. I'll be round again tomorrow with some books to . . .

A gunshot rings out.

Sebastian *walks across the stage. As he passes* **Gabriel**, *he pats him on the arm.*

Sebastian   We still haven't been for that drink.

The farm.

Edwin   Early one morning we get a knock on the door. I think, what's this now. Another load of soldiers? And it is. But they're British.

Jacob   They'd been watching us for days.

Edwin   They're dirty, hungry and exhausted.

Robbie   We'd landed in the middle of the night. Freezing cold, wet. Two days' walk and I still haven't warmed up.

Jacob   We help out with unloading ammunition and rations packs.

Robbie   First lot of Islanders I actually get to meet. Shit, are they all farmers here or what? (*To* **Jacob**.) Hey, give me some good news, will you, mate? Did Leeds United get relegated?

Jacob   Sorry, I don't follow football.

Robbie   Bloody hell. What is this place?

Sally   There's a smell to them. Not them exactly, but the smell of being around them. This harsh, sticky smell of their cookers.

Mary   We make them soup. Lots of it.

Sally   They all smoke while they eat. They stare instead of look.

Mary   Not exactly the Dirk Bogardes one might have imagined. Nonetheless they commend me on the cleanliness of my store.

Edwin   They all seem good lads. In good spirits, even those looking worse for wear. Lots of accents flying about but I can't make head nor tail of any of them.

Robbie   Thanks for the soup, mate.

Edwin   Not a single word.

The town.

Gabriel   I wake one morning to the sound of a soldier having an infected tooth extracted right outside my house. I can't stand this shit anymore. I can't be here. I put on my sneakers, and before I know it I'm outside, running, breathing, fucking breathing again.

Sebastian   I see someone running down the road. At first I think it's a soldier. Stop. Stop, at once! But it's not. It's Gabriel. It's an Islander!

Gabriel   I head down the Ross Road. It's icy but I don't care. Soldiers see me, some even raise their guns but I don't care.

Sebastian   Don't shoot!

John   I hear a commotion and I look outside. It's Gabriel. Gabriel, stop!

Gabriel   I get to the edge of town. The weather is flat and calm. I can see for miles. For the first time in weeks I can see for miles.

The farm.

Sally   A young soldier comes to the back door and asks for a shave and wash. I don't know what to do.

Robbie   I leave my stuff outside, to try and look as much like a normal person as possible and not a bloody soldier barging into her house.

Sally   The bathroom's upstairs, in a locked part of the house.

Robbie   That's fine. I can just shave in the kitchen sink here, if you don't mind? I'm from Manchester.

Sally   I'm from the Falklands.

Robbie   Well, yeah.

Sally   The other soldiers are fine shaving outside.

Robbie   So what? Do you watch them?

Sally   No!

Robbie   It's the hot water. Can't shave in cold, myself. How old are you?

Sally   Why?

Robbie   I'm not chatting you up. I'm just making conversation. I haven't spoken to anyone who's not a squaddie for the last three weeks.

Sally   I'm going on a trip to Gloucester. Have you ever been?

Robbie   Have I fuck. What's in Gloucester?

Sally   I'm going to visit my friend.

Robbie   There's not much more to it than this.

Sally   Well, anyway, I've got jobs to get on with so if you don't mind. . .

Robbie   Busy farm is it?

Sally   Course.

Robbie   What do you do when you're not farming?

Sally   Have parties. Big parties called two-nighters. We play music all night long, as loud as we like.

Robbie   What, like folky fiddle-de-dee stuff?

Sally   No. We get a load of pop music actually because it's easy to ship in.

Robbie   Fair enough.

Sally   Do you want to see my records?

Robbie   Not yet. But when we're coming back through after taking Stanley.

Sally   Take Stanley?

Robbie   Yeah. We start shelling it tomorrow.

Four

The town.

Geoff   Fog. Rain. Winds. A vintage Falklands piss-down. Thankfully we've enough in the cupboards to still make hot toddies.

Sue   We're stopped in the streets much more often. Where we're going, what we're doing. I think it's because of Gabriel's outburst the other day.

Rosie   We're told not to let the kids go down the Darwin Road under any circumstances.

Sebastian   It is just a safety measure.

Rosie   In actual fact it's so they don't see the graves of soldiers who've died from cold and starvation. I overheard the Argentine doctors talking about it.

Sebastian   I filter the letters being sent home. I have to cross out any lines that speak negatively about the conflict. Some men are desperate to surrender and go back home. My God, they could be charged with treason. I'm saving their lives with each strike of my pen.

I don't know how much longer we'll be doing this anyway.

The farm.

Edwin   The British ask for a civilian volunteer to run a message. I'll do it.

Robbie   No offence, mate.

Jacob   I'll go. They ask me to take a message to the commanding officer at Mount Estancia at dawn tomorrow.

Robbie   You've got nothing to worry about. The conflict's pointing that way and you're moving that way.

Sally   You don't have to be brave, Jacob. Just be careful.

The town.

Rosie   The boys help me clean out the chicken coop. We give them a peck about in the front garden while it's quiet.

Sue   I let my two go round and have a look. It's a nice distraction.

Rosie   Then suddenly the sky fills up with harsh light followed by large flashes and loud bangs.

Geoff   That was an air attack in broad daylight.

Rosie   Like fireworks in the afternoon. The kids start cheering.

Sebastian   We hear the shouting and clapping. Some of these soldiers will have lost friends in that attack.

Rosie   They mean nothing by it. It's just the wonder of it.

Sue   But I look at Olly and I think, Christ, maybe my boy did mean it. I find a quiet moment to tell Michael but he doesn't want to hear it. I say, Michael, this is important. He says home is a sanctuary, remember. And it hits me, I've been an absolute idiot. His idea to not talk about the war wasn't for Olly at all, but for him. We're not dealing with this together. He's just sticking his fingers in his ears and what, hoping it all blows over?

Geoff   I hear on the news that Aston Villa have won the European Cup. I think what a cunning trick by the Argentines to try and convince us there's nothing left to live for.

Sebastian   Communications from Buenos Aires are furious, and it's impossible to get a clear idea what's happening. What's evident from the chaos, though, is that we're losing.

Gabriel   They keep two men posted outside my front door. They make jokes about whether next time they should bet on how far I run before the British blow me up.

Sebastian   I'm instructed to reinstall composure in the troops. I admit to the general I don't think I can do it. He looks at me, blankly. Maybe start by reinstalling composure in yourself, *forro*. I go to my quarters and throw up in the sink.

Rosie   Sue, John was meant to come round with some books for the boys. You've not seen him have you?

Sue   No, I haven't.

Rosie   I ask around and eventually find out he's been arrested.

Geoff   For what?

Rosie   They said he didn't have his ID on him while out on the street.

Sebastian   I speak to the monsignor and I suggest he holds some prayer meetings for the soldiers. Something to ground them, something that reminds them of home.

Gabriel   I overhear that a civilian's under arrest. I say through my door, who is it? They say it's the teacher. I come out my house. They try to stop me, I say I'm wearing fucking slip-ons I'm not running anywhere. And I find Sebastian in the church.

Sebastian   I storm down to the police station and I'm shouting at the lieutenant before I'm even through the door. I say if you're going to start imprisoning civilians then we're going to have a fucking uprising on our hands!

Rosie   John's quickly released.

John   I spot Gabriel as I'm led out of the station. He nods to me.

He holds up a hand.

Sebastian   I go back to the church and the monsignor has gone. Called to give the last rites to a boy who had shot himself by accident on the airport road. I hate their word 'accident', I'm sick of how it's used. I go back to my quarters, my stomach is too empty to be sick again, and instead I cry.

Mrs Hargreaves   I doze off in my chair for a minute. Then I hear something. Someone's in the room. Hello?

Gabriel   It's a soldier. He thought the house was empty.

Mrs Hargreaves   You took your time, dear. Oh, hang on. Who are you?

Gabriel   He stands frozen in front of her. With a gun but not threatening. His uniform untucked. Face dirty, lips cracked.

Mrs Hargreaves   Through his bad English and my bad Spanish I gather he's from the Davis Street. It takes me a minute, because I'm thinking I don't know any Argentinian families on Davis . . . And then it hits me, oh yes you're occupying our town. He's freezing cold. He asks for butter.

Sebastian   Butter melts quickly. No evidence of it but high in calories.

Mrs Hargreaves   I give him a whole dinner. I had this ready for my boys, save it going to waste. I wonder what they'd make of their mum making tea for her oppressor!

Gabriel   He tells her she reminds him of his grandmother. He tells her he was in a unit with his best friend from home, but he's now gone.

Mrs Hargreaves   I don't get head nor tail of it. But I let him go on. Anyway, he's polished that plate right off. You look like you needed that.

Gabriel   As a thank you he offers to tidy her garden.

Mrs Hargreaves   He's now talking to me in a different way. He's wanting a response but I don't know what to say.

Gabriel   He says again, tidy her garden. There's a fence knocked over. Piles of trash from the garrison billeted nearby.

John   What she doesn't realise is the hunting rifles I found are buried out there.

Geoff   We thought out of everyone she'd be the least likely to be searched.

Mrs Hargreaves   Oh, my garden.

John   Do I try and cause a distraction?

Geoff   Any noise might alert more soldiers.

Gabriel   He steps out the back, picks up a rake and he's stood right above the loose earth under which the guns are buried.

Mrs Hargreaves   And I see him stood there. Fragile like a bird. I say, oh hang on. I say, my dear, you don't have to do that.

Gabriel (*as soldier*)   No, really. Please. He tries to insist.

Mrs Hargreaves   I don't want to embarrass him. He's got arms like dribbles of milk.

John   Mrs Hargreaves goes up to the soldier and hugs him. And he puts the rake down, kisses her on the cheek and leaves.

Geoff   An absolutely blasted relief. My nerves can't take much more of this.

Sue   Michael decides he wants to do bedtime. He's doing anything other than be in the same room as me at the moment. Later on I find him creeping in the kitchen. Cup of tea? I look him in the eye and say, when was my last day of work? He shakes his head, doesn't understand the question. After this all started, when did I stop working? How much money have we got left? How much peat? When will the kids need new wellies? He says what's this all about. And I say, Michael, I do everything. And yet I go completely unnoticed. To you I'm just an extension of the house, an extension of your needs. He says but I'm ill. And I say I know, and it consumes everything. And I'm the one that always has to have it together, I'm the one who always has to be good. Because your problem is medical and mine is just . . . mine. But I need things, Michael. And he stands there, cup in his hand, and he says, but what do you need? And whether it's dismissive or genuine surprise, his tone hurts me. And so I tell him. About Jimmy. How it started. How long it went on for. Everything. And I can see him quietly spiralling. And I want to apologise, but I don't. And I want to tell him it's not his fault, but I can't. As if all the lies and denials we've been living with are swept away forever in a second. I spend the night in the living room. I've no idea about Michael but I don't get a wink of sleep.

The war zone.

Robbie   Dawn. We move through the landscape towards the mountains that surround Stanley. We get into a tight battle and I kill a man face to face. This is the first time this has happened. I looked him in the eye before I killed him. His eyes were brown. I don't feel anything, but I want to acknowledge that this has now happened.

On a mountain.

Jacob   I get to the top of the ridge and the weather's dense and thick and horrible. They said there'd be someone here to meet me but there's not. I can't see further than about a hundred yards. I can't go back. It's taken too long to not get the job done. And I can't go on, I've no idea what's out that way. Stuck to the spot, in one of the most open bits of land you'd ever see if your life. Then all of a sudden I hear, somewhere, these engine noises. Then out of nowhere this tank bursts out of the mist like a monster. And I think, fuck, this is it. But then they stop, and a guy pops out the top and says, are you looking for us, pal?

The town.

John   It's early morning and the shelling around Stanley begins.

Sue   Big bloody bombs dropping, crashing about all around us.

Geoff   I was lifted six inches off the bed and the cat's gone haywire.

Rosie   How silly to have tears of joy in your eyes when you are being bombed.

Sue   We're one of the houses that don't have a shelter, so we've been told to evacuate. I'm trying to get the kids ready but Michael won't move. Michael! And he's stood there in the bedroom. And I say, Michael, we can't wait for you! And he looks at me with tears in his eyes. And he asks me to promise that once this is over everything will go back to as it was. And I say I can't lie to you anymore, Michael. And he picks up a bag and heads for the door. Mum! The kids are shouting for me now. Mum, we're ready to go!

Rosie   I secure the house, turn off the gas, and lock in the cats and the chickens. Different rooms, obviously.

Sue   We hurry into the gymnasium. We end up being put with Jimmy's family. Which is less than ideal.

Rosie   I grab the bags and get the boys down in the bunker. Still no sign of Geoff, though. Bloody hell. Where are you?

Geoff   I'm ducking and weaving through crowds of soldiers. They're shouting but I keep going.

Sue   The kids are worried about the dog. I think come on, how can you be so naïve?

Geoff   I get to my workshop, open the door and there's the bloody thing. The last bottle of rum on the Island. I rush back to the house.

Rosie   I see Geoff tearing round the corner. He's got the daftest grin on his face. And a bottle of bloody rum. I could throttle you.

John   Three Harriers scream across the sky.

Rosie   Three large black objects fall from the planes and erupt on the ground. Geoff is flung like a doll. I run over to him.

Geoff   I suddenly find myself on the bloody ground. It all went dark for a second. Rosie?

Rosie   You'll be fine, you silly, silly bugger. And I carry him inside.

The farm.

Jacob   I get back to the farm. My eyes are blurry from biking against the snow.

Edwin   Bloody hell, lad. You took your time.

Mary   We were worried sick.

Jacob   Where's Sally?

Sally   Jacob.

They embrace.

Sally   I was so worried about you.

Jacob   I told you I'd be fine.

Sally   Jacob, I've been thinking. If I'd have gone to England when I planned to, then I'd have been away for all this. I'd have been stuck apart from everyone who means something to me. I think you belong in two places. Where you're going but also where you've come from. I still want to go one day.

Jacob   I know you do.

Sally   But I don't want us to fall out over that.

Jacob   We won't.

Sally   Really?

Jacob   I was scared you'd find something there more interesting, more everything, than what's here.

Sally   But I want you to know I won't be going there looking for / a –

Jacob (*interrupts*)   Wait. Because Sally I think that's just a risk I have to live with. You were always going to go and I was never going to be able to keep up. But that's okay. Because the size of your dreams is one of the things I love most about you.

Sally   What?

Jacob   I said the size of your dreams is –

They embrace.

The town.

Sue   It's silent in the gym. The tension between us is masked with feelings about what's happening above. And then Michael mutters, 'What the hell am I going to do?' And Jimmy's wife hugs him and says it'll be over soon.

The war zone.

Sebastian   The biggest garrison is dug in approximately twenty miles from Stanley. On Mount Tumbledown.

Robbie   Rocks jut out of the ground like crooked teeth, catching you off balance, slipping against each other and twisting your ankles. Keep alert, eyes wide open against the ice-cold whipping winds. Watching for foxholes, bunkers, sudden dips and sheer drops. This is the loneliest place in the world, except we're not alone. The enemy has been here for weeks, learnt its secrets, and are now firing upon us as we move upwards. Weaving through the rocks. Taking our time. Attacking, waiting, attacking, waiting. Clearing out trenches and pushing the enemy further and further into the oblivious peak.

Sebastian   The troops are scattered across the hillsides. God grants us some protection with the rock formations. My radio blasts with the pleas for more support, but none is coming.

Robbie   Fatigue sets in. Don't stop. Legs stiffen. Do not fucking stop moving, soldier. The fighting is brutal and hard and tiring because its all at close quarters. Fire, move, fire, stab, move, fire, stab, flash grenade, duck. Cleaning out trenches, pushing them back. There's a lad next to me. Dying but not yet dead. War is fast, but this is taking ages.

Sebastian (*in Spanish*)   Please God, protect me. Please God, think of my mother.

Robbie   We reach the top of the mountain. All active threats neutralised, about half of which are taken alive. The area's mostly occupied by lower-rank soldiers and conscripts.

There's plimsols everywhere. I say what the fuck is it with the trainers? They were told to bring PE kits. They thought this was going to be a drill.

The town.

John   The shells land with a regularity which should make them less shocking, but each explosion turns me sick. And it's about this time –

Rosie   It was about at this time –

Gabriel   Another shell landed.

Geoff   And I remember saying that bloody, that's hit a house. Straight on. Right at the end of the street.

Sue   And Jimmy said a house has been hit. Right opposite us. And I say whose?

Rosie   And it was Mrs Hargreaves.

Robbie *enters the town.*

Robbie   The white flags are already flying as we make it into Stanley. So the movement into town becomes a walk. I say town, it's more like a village.

Sue   British soldiers come into the gym. They ask us to stay put while they secure the area.

Rosie   So we wait, and have to listen to the news reports of what happened in our town.

Gabriel   There's a knock at the door. I freeze. Another knock. It's British soldiers. I answer, because what else can I do? But they just check there's nobody hurt inside.

Geoff   We hear about liberated settlements. Find out Edwin's farm is alright. Thank God. I haven't had a pint with that old sod since the summer.

Gabriel   I look out my door and see Sebastian in a queue of arrested soldiers. He's looking tattered and exhausted.

Sebastian   We're ordered into a line. There's a boy ahead of me, he's shaking. I tell him the British won't torture us, the world is watching. I wonder about back home. Out here these boys were in the front line, in Buenos Aires they will be too. All our lives we have heard that our country will never be whole without Las Malvinas. Well. Now we are the generation that lost it again. A British soldier walks up beside me. He's pointing at a map and telling his friend he can't find the 'facking public works warehouse'. I politely offer directions. I smile as I do. I know this town better than you, my friend.

Rosie   We're eventually allowed out.

Sue   Everything's utterly trashed to bits. Doors kicked in, bullet holes in walls, buildings folded over themselves.

Rosie   I try to go to Mrs Hargreaves's house.

Robbie   It's not safe yet, love.

Rosie   There's an elderly lady.

Robbie   Then we'll find her.

Rosie   Her house was hit.

Robbie   Then we'll find her, love.

John   There wasn't any more he could have said. She was dead and the job of a soldier is not to bring people back to life. Their power only flows in one terrible direction. She would have been the fifteenth dead body he'd seen that day.

Rosie   And yet, I can't accept that. Because this is our town. And things like that don't happen in our town.

Robbie   But now they do. And so what of it?

Geoff   I find myself just wandering through the town, looking at the damage. And I spot a cloud of smoke. Look. The Globe Store's on fire. We go and there's just the shell of her stood there. Poor girl falling apart, inside out. Generations of brickwork, out in the open.

Sue All we can do is watch it.

Geoff And I say, do you want to put that fire out, mate. And he says –

Robbie No point. Best let it burn out.

John After a bit of time we get a flood of letters. Amongst mine is the confirmation that I'm now eligible to take my mid-tour leave to travel South America. Instead I decide to stay and help with the rebuild of the town. I need to see this place back to life. Not because of some patriotic myth, but because of the fact we've all been through this together. We have a history, and I have a feeling I belong. I go to tell Gabriel. But he's gone.

Gabriel I was told the Marine Biology Research Centre would be moving to a new building in town. And it was as I was clearing out my stuff I found an old River Plate mug in the kitchen there. River Plate are my football team from back home. And I think, shit, might it cause offence? There I was already worried about a soccer mug. How was I going to cope every time the conflict gets mentioned? I decided, it was easier to just leave.

John It's a shame that no one could say goodbye.

Rosie We're all invited to a meeting at the town hall.

Sue For the announcement of the Clean Up Stanley campaign. An effort to repair buildings, essential services and remove the debris and rubble from the streets.

Rosie By debris you mean people's houses?

Robbie As soon as we arrive back in England we're all offered the job of returning to help the rebuild. They give us a day to decide, yes or no. I don't get chance to talk to my dad, but I reckon he'd say fuck the dole queue, getting a bit of building experience sounds pretty smart. And anyway those Islands must be the fucking safest place on Earth right now. The last thing I want to do is fight again.

Rosie   There's more military now. We've always had soldiers here but you soon realise there's a big difference between being protected and being defended.

Geoff   They're calling us Fortress Falklands in the news.

Robbie   The locals are alright once you get to know them. A bit odd, but friendly enough. We call them Bennies.

Mary   As in Bennie from *Crossroads*.

Robbie   We're told to stop, the locals don't like it. So we call them Stills.

Mary   As in Still Bennies.

Robbie   Some of the lads don't take to the work. They regret coming back. I don't mind it. I don't know what that says about me and I don't want to pick at that scab, you know? Did I tell you about the penguins, by the way? There are penguins fucking everywhere.

Jacob   I start doing tours around the Islands. Of the hotspots that became famous in the news. Lots of the battle sites and wrecks are just as they were.

Mary   I think it's a daft idea. Imagine a museum about the worst day of your life and you're having to go around it with tourists from Norway.

Rosie   Geoff speaks to forty-odd different reporters from all over the world.

Geoff   There's one journalist who's quit her job at a paper to write a book about us. A book! I don't care. I'm happy to tell anyone about our town. I say I can't tell you the facts, I can just tell you what happened. We're about to tear down the old research centre and I find an old River Plate mug at the back of a cupboard. I've still got it somewhere.

Sally   I tell Mary I'm going to help Dad arrange to buy the farm outright from the landowner. I put together a proposal, tell him it's something we'd like to do before I go to England.

Mary   I say it's a nice idea but maybe hold off telling Edwin. He spends a long time putting down injured cattle. And he's never much in the mood to talk. It's going to take us a generation to replace the sheep slaughtered during the conflict. A sheep's generation, mind you, but still. It'll take years to recover.

Rosie   All the changes, all the attention. It kind of leaves me with an odd feeling, yeah. Almost like it's a performance. Having to show people in Britain that we're worth the fuss, having to justify our existence, you know? They sometimes ask on the news, why do they want to be British anyway? And I think well, we're British because Britain owes us. A hundred years ago they asked our families to come out here. There was nothing. Less than nothing. They sacrificed a way of life to come out here, all alone on a few hostile rocks in the middle of the sea. And they worked hard to made it work. Life here isn't easy, we miss out on a lot of things, and actually, yeah. I'm not grateful to Britain, I think Britain should be grateful to us.

Thatcher *appears.*

Thatcher   Today we meet in the aftermath of the Falklands battle.

Rosie   Or maybe I'm too proud to understand.

Thatcher   Our country has won a great victory and we are entitled to be proud.

Sue   I stop following the news about it, all that's for other people.

Thatcher   This nation had the resolution to do what it knew had to be done – to do what it knew was right.

Sue   Me and Michael have separated. Jimmy and his wife are still together. Maybe they worked it out. People are different, even here.

Thatcher   When we started out, there were the waverers and the fainthearts.

Sue   Part of my job now means I assist with the sales and the break-ups of the farms.

Thatcher   The people who thought that Britain could no longer seize the initiative for herself. The people who thought we could no longer do the great things which we once did.

Sue   And I'm driving out to camp on a job, and it's my first time out since it all started.

Thatcher   Those who believed that our decline was irreversible – that we could never again be what we were.

Sue   There's lots of barbed wire around minefields, blast sites, wrecked aircraft.

Thatcher   What has indeed happened is that now once again Britain is not prepared to be pushed around.

Sue   I stop at Teal Creek and look at the new cemetery for the Argentine dead.

Thatcher   We have ceased to be a nation in retreat.

Sue   There's a nice white fence. The graves all with a cross at the head, with the name on and rank.

Thatcher   Britain found herself again in the South Atlantic.

Sue   On many it just says 'An Argentine Soldier Known to God Alone'.

Thatcher   And she will not look back from the victory she has won.

Edwin   I once knew a guy called Dave Glancy. Dave came here as a sheep farmer from Scotland. Says to me, see, he says if he's going to make a success on these Islands, and by implication if anyone is going to make a success of these Islands, and given I was already here he meant I hadn't, but never mind that, he said he was going to have to eradicate the foxes. Foxes were introduced here by a man called Hamilton in the early 1900s. Dave went about studying these foxes, learning their patterns and habits in hunting and procreating. Anyway, months pass and I see Dave again in Stanley. I ask him how he's getting on. And he tells me of what he thinks was the last fox on the Islands. He tells me he was sitting on his porch and this lonely old tinker just sauntered past his house. Well, Dave Glancy picked up his gun, as calm as the fox was sauntering, and shot it. That was that, so Dave says. Except it was only later that day he noticed the water pressure out his tap being funny. Turns out the shot must've ricocheted and pierced a hole in his supply tank. And he looked at that hole in his tank and says to me, well, Edwin, the problem is, out here, when something gets shot, it stays shot.

Epilogue

The **Remaining Company** *of the town are on stage.*

It's the beginning of spring in our town.

The top blankets are taken off the beds.

Thick coats replaced by thin jackets.

And here come the first buds and blooms of colour where, for a while, colour has not been.

It's almost the start of lambing season.

And everything is back to normal. Except it's not.

Something has happened in our town.

Most things still look as they were, in their right places.

And the missing things, the different things, you notice them too but you try and write that off as life happening.

But really you know why they're gone or why they're different.

It's in the people, the buildings, the feeling of the town. The town's sense of itself.

Memories here are stories that belong to everyone. They cling to the place.

Geoff   Course the thing runs like an old pig, so I'm turning the key and it's snorting and snuffling . . .

Mary   My store, quaint as it may seem, is its own Little England.

Everywhere you turn there's something else.

Sorting her chickens out before she's even had time to put the kettle on for herself. Isn't that how it went?

This town has always thought of itself like any other town in our country.

But that's now been replaced with a story. Of what happened for seventy-four days in the winter of 1982.

It's rare for something to happen to everyone all at once. Like a piece of thread woven right through every single house, drawing together and tying up everybody.

Those in the **Company** *who left in the previous scene now rejoin those already on stage. The* **Company** *then quietly and without fuss begins to reset the stage.*

For some it's a secret.

For others it's the only thing worth talking about. As if to argue it, to win the debate, could solve the feeling.

It is a loss.

A fear.

Not just that.

But also all of that.

There are gaps too.

Sometimes the gaps are quite helpful.

Not broken, because our town is still here. Or maybe always broken, not the thing we thought it was.

And you think how dare books and music still be written after this happened to us.

And even if they paint their houses and grow their gardens, it still happened to us.

It passes through the generations.

And today's Sally will be tomorrow's Sue, who'll be tomorrow's Mrs Hargreaves.

We will tell this story forever.

Because it's ours.

This is our home.

It's all we have.

The **Company** *sings a choral version of 'This Must Be the Place' by Talking Heads*

End.